*Trees & Shrubs
in Garden Design*

Trees & Shrubs in Garden Design

Raymond Foster

DAVID & CHARLES

Newton Abbot   London   North Pomfret (Vt)

Line drawings by Rosemary Wise
Photographs by courtesy of Harry Smith Horticultural
Photographic Collection and Michael Warren

British Library Cataloguing in Publication Data

Foster, Raymond
  Trees and shrubs in garden design.
  1. Gardens—Design 2. Shrubs 3. Trees
  I. Title
  712'.6   SB453

  ISBN 0-7153-8271-3

Typeset by Typesetters (Birmingham) Limited, Smethwick
and printed in Great Britain
by Butler & Tanner Limited, Frome and London
for David & Charles (Publishers) Limited
Brunel House   Newton Abbot   Devon

Published in the United States of America
by David & Charles Inc
North Pomfret   Vermont 05053   USA

Contents

Introduction   7

1   **Planting: Care and Cultivation**   9

2   **Grouping for Maximum Effect**   14

    Plan 1   Groups of three, spreading to a total width of 5m (16ft)   25

    Plan 2   Groups of three, spreading to a total width of 6m (20ft)   32

    Plan 3   Groups of three, spreading to a total width of 7m (23ft)   39

    Plan 4   Groups of four, spreading to a total width of 8m (26ft)   53

    Plan 5   Groups of four, spreading to a total width of 9m (30ft)   63

    Plan 6   Groups of four, spreading to a total width of 10m (33ft)   73

    Plan 7   Groups of five, spreading to a total width of 11m (36ft)   85

    Plan 8   Groups of three, spreading to a total width of 12m (40ft)   96

    Plan 9   Groups of six, spreading to a total width of 13m (43ft)   107

    Plan 10 Groups of five, spreading to a total width of 14m (46ft)   117

    Plan 11 Groups of five, spreading to a total width of 15m (50ft)   126

    Plan 12 Groups of five, spreading to a total width of 16m (53ft)   139

    Plan 13 Groups of four, spreading to a total width of 17m (56ft)   150

    Plan 14 Groups of three, spreading to a total width of 18m (60ft)   158

    Plan 15 Groups of three, spreading to a total width of 19m (62ft)   168

3   **Specimen Trees in Isolation**   178

4   **Summary of Heights and Spreads**   196

    Index   229

Introduction

There are few sadder sights to be seen in the garden than the mutilated stumps and lopped branches of trees which grew larger than their owners anticipated. When purchasing a tree or shrub, it is important to know not only the height, but also the branch spread that can be expected as the crown of foliage develops to its full, unique proportions.

This book includes a selection of over 300 ornamental trees and large shrubs of sizes and shapes to fit gardens of all dimensions, and a choice can be made according to the amount of space available. All the measurements given have been taken from average, well-grown specimens, ignoring records of 'maximum heights'. Some of the subjects are well known and justly popular; others are met with in gardens only rarely, but have been included for their special qualities—not least, their neat shape and manageable size.

Isolated specimen trees can be impressive when correctly sited, and a chapter on their use is included. Most plants, however, are happiest when growing in company, and the 60 small groups described here have been assembled for their compatibility in appearance and performance; flowers and foliage; soil and site. Even the smallest garden need not be without its modest grove, for a plot of no more than 3m by 2.5m (10ft by 8ft) will accommodate the smallest collections of three trees.

Even small trees take a few years to develop their characteristic habit, and the ground beneath them can be covered temporarily with low-growing plants. With each arrangement, a suitable planting accompaniment is suggested. In many cases, these supporting themes will have become so well established that they will continue to flourish long after the trees and shrubs have attained the perfection of maturity.

Raymond Foster

Chapter 1

Planting: Care and Cultivation

A modicum of care at planting time pays handsome dividends in terms of easy establishment and trouble-free growth later on. The rules of good planting are simple and well known, but all too often they are bypassed by busy gardeners as a waste of time and effort.

When trees and shrubs are to be planted in a group especially, their site should be well prepared, weed-free and deeply dug, so that both water and roots can penetrate and move around freely. Individual planting holes should be made large enough to accommodate all the roots; those of open-rooted plants should be arranged evenly spread out, without undue bending, though any extra-long lateral growths, lacking the fine hair-like feeding roots, can be cut off rather than coiled up; the root-ball of container-grown or balled plants should remain intact and undisturbed. The polythene covers of containerised plants should be removed at the time of planting. If the ball of compost is very loose and threatens to crumble, the polythene cover can be left on, provided it is slashed on every side and beneath to allow the growing roots to penetrate into the surrounding soil; but this is not really satisfactory, because these pieces of polythene sheet around the plant can prevent the free movement of moisture through the soil, and may even act as a sump to trap water below ground and drown the feeding roots.

Open-rooted plants should never be left with their roots exposed to the air so that they dry out before planting—even though they are quite dormant—for the fine, hair-like feeding roots are always damaged by drying out, and will fail to start growth in the spring. If they are at all dry, or if the plant looks parched or limp, the roots should be soaked for an hour or two in a pan of water before planting; in the case of container-grown plants, the compost in the container should be watered well before planting. Watering after planting is mainly a matter of settling the soil neatly around the newcomer; if the surface tends to cake when wet, the surrounding area should be hoed or raked over immediately after treading and watering, so that the soil can breathe. It helps the roots to become established if peat and a little slow-acting fertiliser is incorporated in the soil to be replaced in the planting hole; a suitable fertiliser is Enmag, which dissolves slowly and releases plant food over a long period. The fast-acting types of

9

fertiliser normally used for flowers and vegetables, or the lawn, are quite unsuitable for young trees and shrubs—unless, like the hybrid roses, their foremost function is to produce flowers.

Most open-rooted plants can only be planted with safety during their dormant season, which usually lasts from November until April. Containerised and ball-rooted plants, on the other hand, have an equal chance of success whatever their season of planting.

New plants should always be set in the ground at their correct depth—to the soil mark which can be seen at the root collar. It is a common fault to plant too deeply, and this is certainly a major cause of new plants failing to grow properly. Trees which are tall enough to sway in the wind should have a stake inserted at the time of planting—preferably while the planting hole is still open, so that the roots can be arranged around it (or, in the case of containerised subjects, placed as close to the stake as possible), and a type of tie should be used that will allow the stem to expand without restriction as the tree grows.

The immediate effect sometimes required of solitary specimen trees, or the site and combined size of a planned group, will usually suggest the type of tree to be purchased. Largest and dearest among the normal grades is the full standard, which has a clean stem of at least 1.5m (5ft), and usually 2m (6ft), beneath the lowest branch; next in size and price comes the half- or semi-standard, which has a stem of up to 1.5m (5ft); the next category is the bush, without a clearly defined single stem. In the case of some trees, especially pyramidal or columnar ones such as the Lombardy poplar cherry, *Prunus* Amanogawa, there is a further category: the feathered stem, which has small branches growing evenly all the way up. Conifers are normally sold unpruned, with branches and greenery right down to ground level. For planting in groups, they should be allowed to retain this form—at least until they are old enough to start looking unsightly at the base, when they can sometimes be stem-pruned like a broadleaf tree.

As they mature, ornamental trees and shrubs may need crown pruning, an operation which can take several different forms. Pruning with no particular aim in mind should be avoided and, if there is no reason to prune, it should not be done. The reasons for pruning might include:

Encouraging regularity of outline, foliage and flower—e.g. *Ribes sanguineum* can be clipped over like a hedge as soon as spring flowering is finished, hypericums are often clipped hard whilst they are dormant, and potentillas very lightly in the early spring—this type of pruning is akin to topiary;

Retaining a graceful habit and encouraging spring flowers—e.g. *Buddleia alternifolia* should have all the arching shoots which have carried flowers removed as soon as flowering is finished, to allow the uncluttered development of new shoots which are to carry the following year's flowers;

Coppicing to control vigorous growth—e.g. pollarded willows such as *Salix alba* Chermesina, and other shrubs such as the dogwood *Cornus alba*, which produce a fanned crown of brightly coloured young shoots valuable for their winter colour, if they are cut back to the stool every second year; also *Buddleia davidii*, which should be cut hard back in March, allowing new shoots to develop symmetrically and carry the flowers in late summer;

Maintaining the neat proportions of a group and preventing the suppression of smaller plants by larger ones—e.g. many broadleaf trees, such as the weeping willows and the flowering cherries, occasionally need a whole branch removing at their base. The work is usually done in July, as heavy pruning during the winter generally results in a proliferation of unwanted young shoots;

Cleaning by removing the dead, unhealthy or suppressed branches of broadleaf trees and some conifers such as the cedars. Live conifer branches should only be removed during the winter months;

Rejuvenating plants—e.g. hybrid roses, by removing a substantial proportion of the previous season's wood, and sometimes an entire old stem, so that young growth is encouraged to spring from the base and replace it. This type of pruning is usually done early in the spring.

As a precaution against the entry of fungus spores which can quickly cause stem-rot in previously healthy trees and shrubs, large pruning scars are best coated with a hygienic bituminous paint, such as Arbrex.

During the growing season old, well-established groups can demonstrate by the appearance of their leaves if they are healthy or not. Sudden withering and dying of part of the foliage can indicate an attack by the tree-killer disease, honey fungus. As a diagnosis, this can be confirmed by uncovering the stem of an ailing tree at soil level, more or less below the withered leaves, and removing a small piece of bark with the point of a penknife. On infected plants a spreading white fungus similar to dry rot will be seen growing beneath the bark, and

11

this has a distinctive mushroomy smell. The disease is transmitted below ground level, travelling from root to root by means of black, bootlace-like growths. If prompt action is taken, the trees and shrubs in the group can be saved by digging out the topsoil so as to expose as much of the root system as possible, and treating these roots and the surrounding soil with a solution of Armillatox or Bray's Emulsion.

Leaves which appear to be discoloured may be showing signs of nutrient deficiency: pale, generally undersized leaves suggest that the soil has become impoverished, and there is need for a general, slow-acting fertiliser; leaves with a reddish tint and purpling, or more commonly yellowing between the veins, long before autumn coloration is due to appear, are often displaying the symptoms of a lack of magnesium, manganese or zinc, as well as the main plant food elements of potash, phosphate and nitrogen. A spray of foliar feed containing trace elements, plus an application of a slow-acting fertiliser such as Enmag, will cure all these troubles. A foliar spray is always useful, and can be used at any time during the growing season to give the plants a tonic and ensure that there is no lack of the essential elements. With composite groups in particular, the method is convenient for the treatment of selected trees or shrubs, without giving an unwanted boost to others, such as the ground-covering plants.

Large specimen trees can be fed by boring holes a foot or two deep in the ground below the outer fringe of foliage—the area wherein the main feeding roots lie—and topping these holes up with a general fertiliser containing NPK in an evenly balanced ratio. The fertiliser in this case can be of a fast-acting inorganic type such as Growmore, used either dry or in solution, followed up with a thorough soaking to wash it down to the roots. The best way to water a large tree is to leave a hosepipe trickling slowly for a few days; lawn sprinklers can never supply enough.

Large isolated trees are more likely than others to suffer from general nutrient deficiency. Trees growing in the forest, of course, receive the benefit of an annual mulch of dead leaves which returns the goodness to the soil; garden trees normally have to do without this replenishment, and thus suffer from slow starvation. If the design of the garden allows it, leaf mould should be returned in the form of a thick mulch every year; in large gardens with suitably accommodating groups of trees and shrubs, the raw dead leaves themselves can sometimes be swept to the back of the beds and left there to rot—but when this is done there is always the possibility that a contrary wind might lift them all out again, and scatter them where they should not be scattered. Well rotted leaf mould is the best and most natural annual treatment to give trees and shrubs—as smart in appearance as peat, but far cheaper and much more nutritious.

Chapter 2

Grouping for Maximum Effect

Individual plant shapes and foliage textures, and their combined silhouette and overall bulk when viewed as a group, are always of more significance than the colour of their flowers. Flowers are transient by nature, and may have faded after a very few weeks. It would be short-sighted to place trees and shrubs for their flowering qualities alone; of course the colour and season of their flowers must be taken into account, but these are not the primary factors for consideration when planning compatible groups.

More durable than flowers, coloured foliage may last throughout the growing season. In the case of evergreens such as *Elaeagnus pungens* Maculata, the variegated hollies, and some conifers, once planted, the brilliant splash of leaf colour is there to stay. When planning a garden, however, there is often a tendency to overdo the colour; for example, to use a variegated cultivar where the green-leaved type would be better. The effect of this can be to vulgarise the scene. A useful way to approach the question of using coloured foliage is to look at the garden as an artist might plan a landscape painting, by using a basic overall tone, made dark and mysterious at some point where the eye leaves the foreground, and highlighted here and there by a bright shaft of sunlight that draws the eye back to the main scene. In designing with real plants, the basic tone—at least during the summer months—should always be green. Foliage of purple, grey and the darkest yew-like green tends to blur and fade into the background; bright yellows leap out into high relief. That part of a design which is meant to strike the eye first should always carry the lightest, brightest greens and yellows. A glimpse of purple and grey through the foreground foliage lends depth to the layout, and suggests that something interesting might lie beyond.

The most fascinating gardens are often split up into departments. Not too obviously, perhaps, for the trick is always to invite and tempt the visitor; to arouse his curiosity and keep him interested, always expecting to find something special around the next corner—a corner which may well be no more than a strategically placed group of small trees or shrubs, leading from highlight to dark mystery beyond.

This section includes designs for planting arrangements, some of which feature fairly large trees and shrubs; but there is no reason why

14

appropriate schemes should not be duplicated on a reduced scale using smaller plants, for the results will be no less effective. Many shrubs have a strikingly architectural outline, and a selection of these might include:

Aucuba japonica varieties, evergreen with several good leaf variegations, for sun or shade, densely compact, rounded, 2–3m (6–10ft) high × 2m (6ft) across;

Berberis spp. and vars., finely foliaged, prickly, with attractive yellow flowers in the spring, especially Barbarossa, with red berries in the autumn, arching, 1.5–2m × 2.5m (5–6ft × 8ft); Bountiful, with heavy crops of red berries, arching, 1m × 2m (3ft × 6ft); *B. darwinii*, evergreen, with excellent flowers, arching, 1.5–2m × 2m (5–6ft × 6ft); *B. julianae*, dense evergreen foliage, domed, 3m × 2.5m (10ft × 8ft); *B. × stenophylla*, evergreen, flowering profusely, arching, 2.5m × 2.5m (8ft × 8ft); *B. wilsoniae*, with good berries, rounded, 1m × 1m (3ft × 3ft);

Buddleia spp. and vars.—*B. alternifolia*, which is included in one of the main designs, can be grown as a shrub or a small tree, with purple spring flowers, weeping, 3m × 3m (10ft × 10ft); *B. davidii* has numerous varieties with late summer flowers ranging from white through mauve to purple-red, fan-shaped if cut hard back in March each year, 2.5m × 2.5m (8ft × 8ft); *B. globosa*, with orange flower balls in the spring, is less symmetrical and makes an upright dome, 3m × 2.5m (10ft × 8ft);

Camellia spp. and vars., evergreen, numerous cultivars with beautiful flowers in winter and spring, all need a fairly acid, peaty soil, very variable in size and shape, but often neatly domed, about 2m × 1.5m (6ft × 5ft);

Ceratostigma willmottianum, with bright blue flowers in late summer and autumn, soft foliage, rounded, 1m × 1m (3ft × 3ft);

Chaenomeles speciosa vars., mostly with red flowers in the spring, spreading, 2m × 3m (6ft × 10ft);

Cornus alba vars., usually included for winter colour—the young shoots have red bark and are cut back every second spring, fan-shaped, 3m × 3m (10ft × 10ft);

Corylus avellana Aurea, the yellow-leaved hazel, can be cut back every few years to produce a fan shape, normally spreading, 2.5m × 3.75m (8ft × 12ft);

Corylus maxima Purpurea, the purple-leaved filbert, ideal for planting behind the yellow-leaved hazel to make a beautiful woodland combination, spreading, 4.5m × 5.5m (15ft × 18ft);

Buddleia globosa. This South American spring flowering shrub makes an upright dome, in contrast with the weeping *B. alternifolia*

Euonymus japonicus, typically a dark evergreen, with several good variegated forms, for sun or shade, rounded, 3.75m × 3.75m (12ft × 12ft);

Forsythia × intermedia Lynwood, with profuse yellow flowers in the spring, arching-spreading, 2m × 3m (6ft × 10ft);

Genista hispanica, Spanish gorse, a spiny plant for dry sunny sites, covered with yellow flowers in the spring, mounding, 60cm × 1m (2ft × 3ft);

Hebe spp. and vars., shrubby veronica, evergreen, neatly compact with white or mauve flowers in the summer, useful for sunny sites, spreading mounds up to 1m × 2m (3ft × 6ft);

Hypericum spp. and vars., free-flowering, with neat, glaucous-green foliage, especially *H. androsaemum*, the tutsan, with small yellow flowers throughout the summer and a succession of red and black berries, domed, 75cm × 50cm (30in × 20in); Hidcote, a hybrid with large yellow flowers in the late summer, domed, 1.5m × 2m (5ft ×

16

Kerria japonica

6ft); *H. calycinum,* the rose of Sharon, to continue the theme at ground level, with large yellow flowers in the summer, spreading, up to 50cm (20in) high;

Kerria japonica, with yellow flowers in the spring, makes a green-stemmed arching fan, 1.5m–2m × 2m (5–6ft × 6ft);

Philadelphus spp. and vars., mock orange; Virginal has sweetly scented double white flowers in the summer and makes an upright dome, 3m × 2.5m (10ft × 8ft);

Potentilla fruticosa vars., the shrubby cinquefoils, free-flowering, with neat grey-green foliage; especially the hybrid Elizabeth with bright yellow flowers throughout the summer, domed, 1m × 1m (3ft × 3ft); Katherine Dykes, with primrose-yellow flowers, domed, 2m × 1m (6ft × 3ft);

Prunus laurocerasus, the common laurel, a rather shapeless vigorous evergreen with large, glossy, leathery leaves, and white flowers in the spring, valuable as a heavy screen, spreading, 6m × 8m (20ft × 26ft);

Prunus lusitanica, the Portugal laurel, a darker evergreen than the common laurel, with smaller leaves, white flowers in early summer, grows well in poor, chalky soils, rounded, 5m × 5m (16ft × 16ft);

Rhododendron spp. and vars., dark evergreen foliage and striking spring flowers, for acid, peaty soils in semi-woodland conditions; small and neatly compact varieties up to 1m (3ft) high include Cilpinense, with pale pink flowers in March and April; Little Bert, with scarlet flowers in April; larger varieties neatly compact and domed up to 2m (6ft), broader than high, include Britannia, one of the best, with dark red flowers in May; Doncaster, with red flowers in May; Goldsworth Yellow, with yellow flowers in May; vigorously upright varieties up to 3m (10ft) include Beauty of Littleworth, with white, crimson-spotted flowers in May; Blue Peter, with violet flowers in May; Cynthia, very hardy, with crimson flowers in May; Pink Pearl, a very popular variety with pink flowers in May;

Ribes sanguineum vars., the flowering currant, a neatly compact plant, especially if clipped every year in early summer; the typical species has pink flowers in the spring, densely domed, 2m × 2m (6ft × 6ft); King Edward VII is a favourite variety with crimson spring flowers, domed, 1.5m × 1.5m (5ft × 5ft); Pulborough Scarlet has flowers more crimson than scarlet, domed, 2m × 2m (6ft × 6ft); Carneum has flesh pink flowers in the spring, domed, 2m × 2m (6ft × 6ft);

Rosmarinus officinalis vars., rosemary, evergreen with greyish-green white-backed leaves and blue flowers in the spring; Miss Jessop's

Philadelphus Virginal. Sweetly scented double white flowers are carried in the summer by this favourite variety of the mock orange

Variety makes an upright dome, 2m × 1m (6ft × 3ft); Severn Sea is arching, 50cm × 1m (20in × 3ft);

Sambucus nigra Aurea, the golden elder, very hardy and rather coarse, ideal for a group to be seen at a distance, rounded, 4m × 4m (13ft × 13ft);

Senecio greyi, grey-leaved evergreen with yellow daisy flowers in the summer, spreading mound, 75cm × 2m (30in × 6ft);

Skimmia japonica vars., evergreen with white spring flowers, all good in the shade, domed, 1m × 1m (3ft × 3ft);

Viburnum opulus, a vigorous shrub with maple-like leaves and flat white flower heads in the summer, spreading, 4m × 6m (13ft × 20ft);

Senecio greyi

the snowball bush *V.o.* Sterile is a more compact variety, with conspicuous white snowball flowers in the summer, spreading, 2.25m × 4m (7ft × 13ft);

Viburnum plicatum tomentosum, horizontally tiered branches with white flowers in the spring, spreading, 4m × 6m (13ft × 20ft); the variety Mariesii is an improved form with very horizontal branching and abundant white flowers in the spring, one of the most valuable shrubs for building small groups, spreading, 3m × 5m (10ft × 16ft);

Weigela spp. and vars., with red, white or pink flowers in the spring, arching, 2m × 2m (6ft × 6ft).

Among the smaller conifers commonly seen in gardens, the prostrate spreading junipers and the taller, fan-shaped pfitzer juniper have been planted so frequently over the past few years that they have

Sambucus nigra Aurea, the golden elder, has a good colour but is somewhat coarse; ideal for inclusion in a group to be seen at a distance

Viburnum plicatum tomentosum Mariesii, with its horizontally tiered branches, is one of the most valuable shrubs for building small groups

perhaps begun to pall, although they fully justify their use and remain unbeatable in the context of a rock garden. The case is similar with some other dwarf conifers, such as those varieties of Lawson's cypress that remain below a metre or two in height. On the rock garden they are charming; but their great disadvantage when used in free-standing groups is their extremely slow growth. A few of the taller conifers suitable for general garden use are listed later in the book as specimen trees; others are included in the groups that follow.

Assembled for their compatibility in appearance and performance, flowers and foliage, soil and site, these groups are arranged progressively according to their eventual overall branch spread:

Plan 1   Groups of three, spreading to a total width of 5m (16ft)
Spring flowerers for a sunny spot (p.25)
Spring flowers and evergreen foliage (p.28)
Summer flowers for a sheltered garden (p.29)

Plan 2   Groups of three, spreading to a total width of 6m (20ft)
          A flowering group for the woodland garden (p.34)
          Spring, summer and autumn (p.35)
          A berrying group (p.37)

Plan 3   Groups of three, spreading to a total width of 7m (23ft)
          Cherry blossom with a sea-green conifer (p.39)
          Cherry blossom with a blue conifer (p.43)
          A colourful succession (p.45)
          A crabapple group (p.46)
          A spring flowering and berrying group (p.47)
          A group for winter colour (p.48)
          A winter and spring flowering group (p.51)

Plan 4   Groups of four, spreading to a total width of 8m (26ft)
          Maples and conifers (p.53)
          A spring flowering group (p.58)
          A graceful combination (p.60)
          A distinguished choice (p.62)

Plan 5   Groups of four, spreading to a total width of 9m (30ft)
          A maple grove (p.63)
          Some shapely berrying trees (p.66)
          A *Prunus* collection for spring display (p.68)
          An unusual group of contrasting beauty (p.69)

Plan 6   Groups of four, spreading to a total width of 10m (33ft)
          An unusual woodland garden group (p.73)
          A colourful group from spring to autumn (p.77)
          A group with long-lasting ornamental fruits (p.83)
          A collection of small maples (p.84)

Plan 7   Groups of five, spreading to a total width of 11m (36ft)
          A screening group for a sunny garden (p.85)
          An unusual spring flowering group (p.88)
          For year-round beauty (p.91)
          A bold display of colour (p.93)

Plan 8   Groups of three, spreading to a total width of 12m (40ft)
          A collection of crabapples (p.96)
          Three rare berrying trees (p.101)
          Three unusual American trees (p.102)
          A striking blend of foliage (p.103)
          A beautiful group at all seasons (p.106)

Plan 9   Groups of six, spreading to a total width of 13m (43ft)
A representative collection of maples (p.107)
Woodlanders with white flowers and handsome foliage (p.111)
Whitebeams and rowans with striking berries (p.114)

Plan 10   Groups of five, spreading to a total width of 14m (46ft)
Collection of magnolias I (p.119)
Collection of magnolias II (p.122)
Hardy ornamentals for a tough site (p.124)

Plan 11   Groups of five, spreading to a total width of 15m (50ft)
Colour and beauty throughout the year (p.126)
Spring blossom and contrasting foliage (p.131)
Spring flowers and blending foliage (p.135)

Plan 12   Groups of five, spreading to a total width of 16m (53ft)
Quiet colours with blending foliage textures (p.139)
A striking blend of colours (p.143)
A group for blossom and berry (p.144)
With the accent on pink and red (p.147)

Plan 13   Groups of four, spreading to a total width of 17m (56ft)
A selection of flowering cherries (p.150)
A long season of colour (p.155)
Spring flowers and winter colour (p.156)

Plan 14   Groups of three, spreading to a total width of 18m (60ft)
Spring flowering cherries (p.160)
Combining winter and spring flowering (p.162)
Superb flowers and striking foliage (p.163)
Flowers and autumn berries (p.166)
A beautiful group at all seasons (p.167)

Plan 15   Groups of three, spreading to a total width of 19m (62ft)
Subtle spring blossom and dramatic foliage (p.168)
Magnificent blossom and contrasting foliage (p.171)
Bright autumn fruits (p.173)
A woodland display of green and white (p.174)
A spectacular group (p.176)

Plan 1
Groups of three, spreading to a total width of 5m (16ft)

A simple and compact little arrangement which looks equally attractive from any angle. The actual area required on the ground measures 3m (10ft) by 2.5m (8ft).

Spring flowerers for a sunny spot

From left to right: *Prunus* Umineko
Prunus Taizanfukun
Prunus Cheal's Weeping Cherry

These three flowering cherries are completely hardy and will grow in any soil, provided they are given a reasonably open, sunny site. Heavy overshading will spoil their symmetry and inhibit flowering.

Theirs is a charming but refined colour scheme of pink and white, commencing in March and lasting through April. First of the three to flower, before the leaf buds break, is Cheal's Weeping Cherry, and this is soon covered right down to the ground with double blossom of a somewhat mauvy pink. Before this is full blown, the small upright cherry Umineko opens its pure white petals—the numerous flowers are single, and delicate enough to relieve any tendency to heaviness which such a wealth of double pink blossom near ground level might produce. These white flowers are followed in quick succession by the taller cherry Taizanfukun in palest pastel pink—a subtle combination, all set off beautifully by the young leaves which now, by late April, are starting to unfurl and display rich shades of bronze, copper and fresh green.

During the summer months the foliage, typical for cherries, is a lush, dark green, and all three trees colour bright yellow, amber and russet in the autumn, before the leaves finally fall.

Such naturally compact trees will rarely need pruning. Taizanfukun has a dense, twiggy crown of branches, and Umineko is neat and shapely, but the lowest branches can be removed from either or both of them as they mature, especially if small plants are to be grown beneath their canopies, for this heavy pruning—called raising the crown—will let in a great deal of light that was excluded before and, incidentally, ensure that their composite silhouette is restricted to the planned dimensions. A weeping tree can be said to have an upside down crown and, if Cheal's Weeping Cherry threatens to outgrow its site, the same procedure can be followed in reverse, and the heaviest, topmost branches can be removed whenever they start to arch too

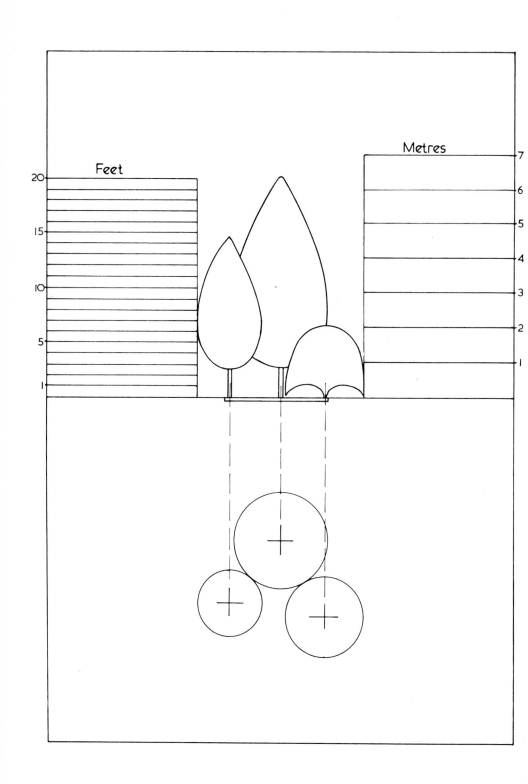

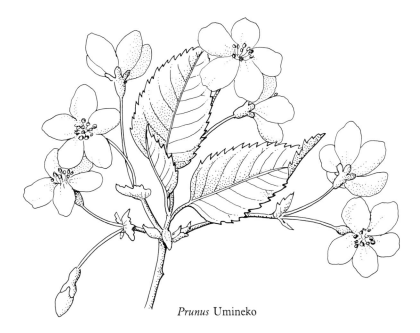

Prunus Umineko

enthusiastically. These large branches must be removed cleanly to their base, and the work should be done preferably in July.

If there is too much overshadowing of this group from tall trees growing nearby, while they will survive such a situation, they may tend to lose their compact shape and become gappy and rangy, so that the planned effect will be lost. Cheal's Weeping Cherry can be planted fairly close to a wall or another tree, so that it grows one sided—this could be a deliberate policy where space is very restricted, provided the backing is solid enough to support it. Wooden fences tend to be weakened and eventually pushed over if a tree crown is constantly pressing against them, as it is liable to do during windy weather.

Cheal's Weeping Cherry is often said to be the same plant as the Japanese Kiku-shidare Sakura, and the two are, at any rate, much confused. Some nurseries grow a distinctly heavier, taller and wider-spreading tree, with brighter pink blossom, and this I take to be Kiku-shidare Sakura. Other growers produce a slenderer plant with flowers of a deeper mauve-pink, and this is probably the original Cheal's Weeping Cherry. Where the dimensions are not of great importance, a tree purchased under either name will be equally suitable for this arrangement.

Plan 1—Groups of three trees, spreading to a total width of 5m (16ft)

Spring flowering bulbs such as the crocuses and chionodoxas always look especially beautiful around the roots of these little trees, but, even before the leaves appear, the weeping cherry has so solid an umbrella of branches that few plants are able to do well beneath its shade. If the group is sited very near to the house, or bordering a path so that it can be seen at close quarters, and the ground beneath Cheal's Weeping Cherry seems too bare to leave unclothed, one plant that should succeed in this confined place is the winter aconite, *Eranthis hyemalis*, for this useful little bulb lies dormant during the summer months and produces its leaves during the winter, when the light intensity below the branches is at its maximum. It will provide a very cheerful drift of bright buttercup-yellow flowers in late winter and early spring, before the first of the cherry blossom opens.

Spring flowers and evergreen foliage

From left to right: *Juniperus chinensis*
     Malus × *sublobata*
     Prunus Hilling's Weeping Cherry

This second group will grow in sunny sites anywhere, and has no special soil preferences. The juniper should be allowed to retain its branches to ground level.

The succession of white and pink spring blossom, starting early in April with Hilling's Weeping Cherry clothed down to the ground in pure white, followed within a fortnight by the pale pink of the little crabapple *Malus* × *sublobata*, is accentuated this time by the dark grey-green, finely textured foliage of the Chinese juniper.

These two hybrid trees form, with the juniper, a very compactly shaped group which will rarely tend to grow out of bounds. Hilling's Weeping Cherry has a narrower outline than Cheal's Weeping Cherry or Kiku-shidare Sakura, and its overall height depends primarily on the length of the original standard stem that formed a budding stock, or, if a different method of propagation was used, on the length of shoot that was trained in the nursery to grow upright and become a stem. Once firmly established, it shows little inclination to mound upwards over the years—a tendency to which many weeping trees are prone; any upward-leading shoot which develops can be cut off at its base. Eventually, it is true, branches will start to arch outwards a little too strongly and increase the effective spread of the crown, but these also can easily be removed as they appear. Similarly, as the tree ages, new growths will lengthen the weeping branches until they are trailing along the ground, and these too should be curtailed. When this stage of growth is reached—the tree by then will be many years old—some of the oldest branches may be removed annually in a light pruning operation, allowing young shoots to take their place, as happens with rose bushes. Winter pruning tends to result in a proliferation of undesirable twiggy growth, and trees pruned during the spring and early summer may suffer a debilitating loss of sap through bleeding; late summer is the best season to prune small flowering cherries such as these.

When the crabapple blossom fades, tiny apples start to develop until they turn yellow in the late summer, and often remain to decorate the bare branches after the leaves have fallen. Few nurseries grow *Malus × sublobata*, and enquiries for it should encourage them to stock it, for, with its neat, military stance, this little Japanese hybrid crabapple has a shape which is very useful in small gardens, and a degree of hardiness that enables it to thrive in any sunny position.

The yellow-foliaged juniper *Juniperus chinensis* Aurea could be used instead of the wild grey-green type, and this would help to provide a little colour during the quiet season, but the yellow form keeps its colour better in at least partial shade—a situation which does not really suit the weeping cherry.

This group has a space to the forefront which can well accommodate herbaceous or shrubby plants of the appropriate height, preferably with foliage that will form a contrast and flowers that will complement the blossom before it fades. The bergenias have neatly rounded leaves backed with a crimson tinge, a shape and colour that suits these small trees admirably, and the variety *Bergenia* Crimson Glow produces its crimson flowers in late April and May. After the cherry and the crab have shed their leaves, the bergenia foliage turns crimson and purple, and remains to brighten the winter scene.

Summer flowers for a sheltered garden

From left to right: *Eucryphia glutinosa*
                      Stewartia koreana
                      Salix caprea Kilmarnock

In this unusual group, an exotic touch is brought to the garden by the summer flowers of eucryphia and stewartia, and the homely weeping goat willow Kilmarnock is bright with catkins in the early spring. They need a sheltered garden with soil that is free from lime.

Salix caprea Kilmarnock is a variety of the wild British goat willow,

Juniperus chinensis

and able to grow almost anywhere, but the other two are less easily pleased. *Eucryphia glutinosa* is a South American tree that appreciates the woodland type of environment found in a lightly shaded garden with a loamy, slightly acid soil. *Stewartia koreana* which, as its name implies, comes from Korea, also likes to have its roots in a moist, shady place. This group will be ideally situated if their roots can be shaded while their crowns are able to bask in the sunlight—a combination of circumstances which often occurs unplanned when tall trees or buildings are close by.

Salix caprea Kilmarnock

Both the upright trees become laden during July and August with gorgeous 6cm (2½in) round-petalled white flowers with prominent yellow anthers. The miniature weeping willow is at its best in late winter and early spring when it is decked with large yellow catkins, for it is a male plant. There is another, less pendulous variety of weeping goat willow which is female, sometimes known as Weeping Sally, and this displays the familiar silvery 'palms'.

All three have neat leaves in blending shades ranging from the dark shining green of the eucryphia to the soft grey sage of the willow. In the autumn, the eucryphia and the stewartia display bright colours before the leaves fall, although, in mild winters, the former sometimes keeps its leaves intact if the garden is well sheltered from cold winds. It also has a very ornamental, peeling bark which looks charming if the group has been sited so as to catch any winter sunshine.

Any plant expected to run around the stems and roots of these small trees will need to be one that enjoys the shade. If it has a purple tinge to its leaf colour, this will stress the subtle variations in green and the clear whiteness of the summer flowers. Such a plant is the bugle, *Ajuga reptans*, in one of its varieties; Burgundy Glow and Multicolor

31

A close view of the summer flowers of *Eucryphia glutinosa*. This South American woodland tree needs a sheltered, lightly shaded site and an acid, loamy soil

have ground-covering leaves, their basic green variegated with shades of purple, crimson, bronze and pink, and, in the nature of a bonus, spikes of not unattractive blue flowers appear early in the summer.

Plan 2
Groups of three, spreading to a total width of 6m (20ft)

A similar arrangement to Plan 1, but with a more rotund effect, and with greater scope for the use of low carpeting plants and bulbs. These

Plan 2—Groups of three trees, spreading to a total width of 6m (20ft)

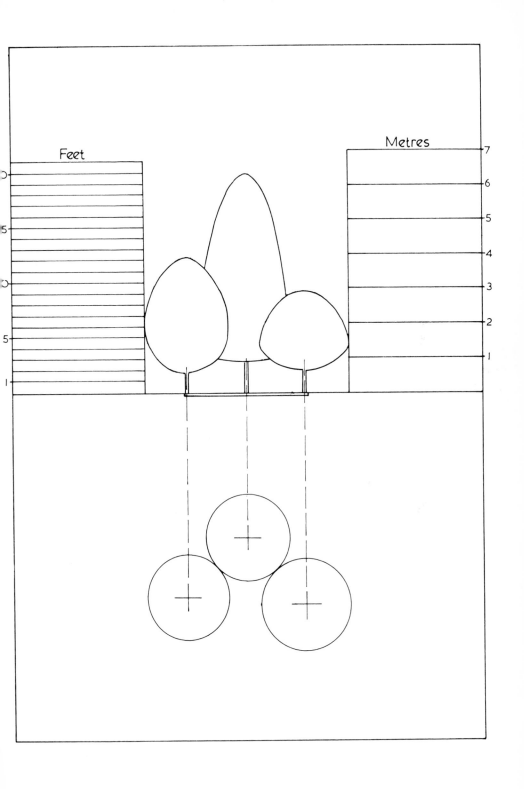

Feet

Metres

7

6

5

4

3

2

1

groups will look equally effective when viewed from the front or from the rear. Actual ground area required: 4m (13ft) by 2.25m (7ft).

A flowering group for the woodland garden

From left to right: *Magnolia dawsoniana*
Eucryphia × *nymansensis* Nymansay
Magnolia cordata

A cool woodland atmosphere is right for this group, and the soil must be moist, peaty and free from lime.

These beautiful little trees have varied origins: *Magnolia dawsoniana* comes from China, a hardy plant introduced to the West early in the 20th century; *M. cordata* is the yellow-flowered magnolia from Georgia and the adjoining states of America, where it is rare in the wild, although it has been cultivated for centuries; and the eucryphia originated as a hybrid between two Chilean trees.

In flower they are all eye-catching. The Chinese magnolia has the disadvantage of not producing its huge pink spring flowers until it is several years old—there is an obvious case here for purchasing rather older plants than nurseries usually sell. It might be persuaded to flower at an earlier age if a little sulphate of potassium is applied in the late summer and worked into the ground around its roots. Meanwhile, however, it is very attractive in foliage, with its large, leathery, bright green leaves, and its distinctively neat shape means that these early flowerless years are not without ornamental value.

The other two trees flower simultaneously in August and September and complement each other: the eucryphia with a blanket of pure white, broad-petalled flowers; the American *Magnolia cordata* with narrow, buttercup yellow petals—less spectacular than *M. dawsoniana*, but with the advantage of flowering while the tree is still young.

Eucryphia × *nymansensis* Nymansay was first raised in the famous English garden of Nymans in Sussex. It is said to grow more rapidly and to be marginally more hardy than the hybrid *E.* × *nymansensis* of which it is a selected form, but, in any case, it does well in southern Britain and the milder states of America. When grown in warm regions or very sheltered gardens, it often keeps its leaves the year round, but becomes completely deciduous in hard winters.

Polygonum campanulatum is a good herbaceous plant to run around the stems of this group, for it thrives in the shade and spreads quickly without becoming too invasive, producing clusters of pinkish-white flowers that show up well during the summer months.

Magnolia dawsoniana

Spring, summer and autumn

From left to right: *Malus × zumi*
                       Sorbus Embley
                       Aesculus discolor

This group of trees will grow in any type of soil, on any site that is not heavily shaded.

The first flowers in this interesting selection make their appearance in mid May with the hybrid crabapple, *Malus × zumi*. Its buds are of a delicate shade of rose, so that it seems as if it is about to open pink; but this colour is limited to the petal reverse and, as soon as the flowers open fully, there is no doubt that they are pure white, and also very fragrant. *Sorbus* Embley, a beautiful rowan of uncertain origin, produces its clusters of white flowers at the end of May, and these last well into June, by which time the small buckeye *Aesculus discolor* has started to open its bicolour red and yellow candles.

A. discolor produces the domed, inverted pudding basin silhouette typical of the horse chestnut genus, but on a small, shrubby scale. It is a native of the rich, moist river valleys of the southern United States

Sorbus Embley

and, in this habitat, it is said to reach a fair size. In cooler parts of America and in Britain, however, growth is much shrubbier and more compact, and it is not likely to exceed the bounds of this scheme. The species itself is not always available from nurseries, but it is one of the parents of a few hybrid forms, among them the very beautiful Harbisonii, which has scarlet flower spikes, and Induta, whose amber flowers last well through June, and both of these are normally stocked by the larger growers.

As summer progresses, *Malus* × *zumi* is bedecked with tiny bright red apples—or large berries—and the rowan berries are also developing until, by September, they are a brilliant glossy orange, for Embley is one of the brightest of its genus in fruit.

Foliage harmony among the three is marked, for each is distinct yet complementary: the striking foliage of the buckeye, whose 15cm (6in) palmate leaves are a dark glossy green on their upper surfaces and downy grey beneath; the dark, rounded or occasionally lobed crabapple leaves; and the small, almost feathery leaves of *Sorbus* Embley, which colour brightly in the autumn with fiery tints of red, orange and yellow.

A useful plant to associate with this group is the tutsan, *Hypericum androsaemum*, for its low, rounded bushes accentuate perfectly the larger domed shapes of the trees, and the colours blend well, with numerous small yellow flowers during the summer, and attractive red and black berries in great profusion. Once established, they seed themselves readily and can form a weed-proof cover.

A berrying group

From left to right: *Sorbus cashmiriana*
Sorbus aucuparia Sheerwater Seedling
Sorbus chamaemespilus

This little group will thrive in all types of soil and sites, provided they are not too heavily shaded, even in places that are exposed to cold winds or to industrial and highway pollution.

Trees of the genus *Sorbus* are not usually noted for their flowers; these are pleasant enough, but they rarely draw much attention when they are out in May and June, although they often appear in great profusion, for their slightly greenish shade of white tones with the young foliage and makes them rather inconspicuous. This is true of Sheerwater Seedling, a selected variety of the British mountain ash, but the other two trees in this group have pink flowers, which strike an unusual note.

Sorbus cashmiriana, a mountain ash from Kashmir, has numerous saw-toothed leaflets of a fresh, bright green. *S. chamaemespilus*, on the other hand, belonging as it does to the whitebeam section of the genus,

has rounded, toothed leaves of a shining dark green which stresses the lighter green of the tiny rowan leaves. The delicate pink flowers of these two trees are massed in large, conspicuous clusters, so that one's attention is drawn in the early summer to the tall cone of greenish white blossom rising from a cloud of pink.

If the flowering display at the beginning of June is pretty, the subsequent show of berrying in late summer and autumn is quite spectacular: *S. chamaemespilus* dripping with crimson red at the branch tips; Sheerwater Seedling with huge bunches of bright shining orange berries; and *S. cashmiriana* with drooping clusters in clear mistletoe white. White berries in the genus *Sorbus* usually last longer on the tree than the more typical red as birds seem to leave them alone, and *S. cashmiriana* often remains garlanded with these white clusters long after signs of summer have passed and the trees stand leafless.

S. cashmiriana is from the western Himalayas, and *S. chamaemespilus* is also a mountain species, from Europe; both are very hardy and well able to grow in less than ideal conditions. *S. aucuparia* itself is the familiar British rowan, which thrives in bleak sites over much of Europe, and has been introduced into the United States and Canada where it is now so much at home that it has naturalised itself in many places. Sheerwater Seedling is a form of the species which was selected for its very neat proportions and bright fruits.

The beautiful foliage of this group can be dramatised by planting some of the herbaceous bronzeleafs nearby. One of the best for the purpose is *Rodgersia aesculifolia*, which has conspicuous horse chestnut-like leaves with 25cm (10in) leaflets, and large white flower clusters during the summer.

Plan 3
Groups of three, spreading to a total width of 7m (23ft)

Arranged for maximum contrast of form with simplicity. All three trees can be seen equally well from every side. The actual ground area required for this plan is 3.5m (12ft) by 2.5m (8ft).

Cherry blossom with a sea-green conifer

From left to right: *Prunus incisa* Moerheimii
Chamaecyparis lawsoniana Pottenii
Prunus Asano

(Opposite) Sorbus aucuparia Sheerwater Seedling

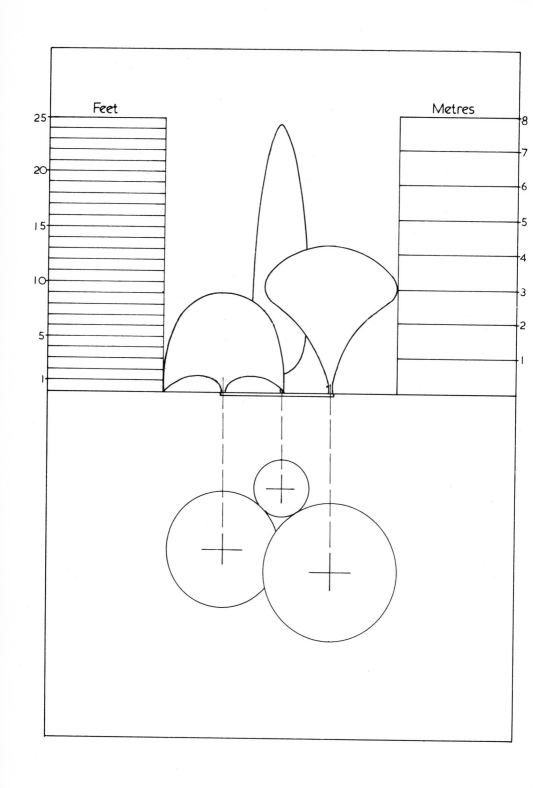

Feet

Metres

25

20

15

10

5

1

8

7

6

5

4

3

2

1

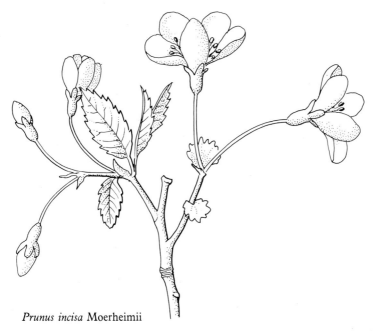

Prunus incisa Moerheimii

These are very hardy trees that need full sunshine to retain their symmetrical silhouettes. They will grow in any reasonable soil, provided it does not dry out too drastically in the summer. The cypress Pottenii should be allowed to keep all its branches and foliage down to ground level.

Prunus incisa is the Japanese Fuji cherry, a favourite not only in gardens and Japanese paintings, but also as a bonsai subject, for it is well suited to this ancient Japanese art of tree dwarfing, and always drapes itself gracefully without the need for drastic restraint. Its variety Moerheimii has flowers of the palest pink, appearing well before the leaves open, often as early as the last week in March, and persisting into April.

To match this early flowering season, *Prunus* Asano is spectacular in early April too, absolutely laden with large, double, deep pink flowers which are at their best just as the bronzy young leaves are starting to open. In full summer leaf, both cherries are a healthy dark green, though excessive dryness at the roots sometimes results in a yellow tinge to their foliage—a precursor of the beautiful autumn tints they usually develop.

Chamaecyparis lawsoniana Pottenii has the softest foliage of any variety of Lawson's cypress, with closely crowded feathery leaves of a

Plan 3—Groups of three trees, spreading to a total width of 7m (23ft)

rather glaucous sea-green. It is normally multi-stemmed under its foliage and, once the tree has passed a height of about 2m (6ft), it is sensible, as a precaution against flopping and splitting open when weighed down with snow and lashed by winter gales, to encircle it with garden tying wire, in loops about 50cm (20in) apart. By teasing out the leaf sprays the wire can be arranged so that it does not show and, anyway, after a season's growth it will be completely hidden beneath the foliage. The soft texture of Pottenii is ideal as a foil for cherry blossom, and it is just as effective in countering any impression of heaviness or coarseness that the rather large *Prunus* leaves might convey.

Flowering cherries cast quite a heavy shade during the summer months, and *P. incisa* Moerheimii shades almost as heavily as the true weepers of the Japanese group, while Asano is perhaps slightly lighter than average as a shade-caster. Spring bulbs are some of the best plants to associate with them, for their flowering can be over and done with before the tree leaves are fully developed, and the bulb foliage, where this is persistent, is able to grow lushly in the subdued light beneath the cherry canopy. Blue flowers often seem to blend best with the soft pink shades of the blossom—grape hyacinths, bluebells and the early *Anemone blanda*.

If planting space is available to the rear of this group, some of the prostrate junipers could be planted around the feet of Pottenii; plants such as *Juniperus horizontalis* Bar Harbor or Coast of Maine, with their mat of greyish-green foliage.

Cherry blossom with a blue conifer

From left to right: *Prunus avium* Pendula
Cupressus glabra Pyramidalis
Prunus Hisakura

This beautiful group needs a dryish soil of any type—quite strongly alkaline soils are suitable—in a sunny but moderately sheltered garden, sited for preference on a slight slope, so that cold air can drain away. The smooth cypress, of course, will retain its foliage to ground level while still a young tree, but it is often desirable to prune the true cypresses to semi-standard height as they mature.

The wild cherry of Britain and Europe is *Prunus avium*, well known as a woodland and roadside tree, and greatly admired every spring for

(Opposite) Chamaecyparis lawsoniana Pottenii is often mistaken when young for a dwarf rock garden tree. This conifer is capable of attaining 12m (40ft) or more

its pretty white blossom. It is a handsome tree throughout the seasons, with its grey, green and mahogany bark and quite spectacular autumn leaf colours. Its weeping variety Pendula occurs in nature from time to time, and nursery-bred specimens will have descended from slightly differing forms, so that bought trees of this name may vary one from another. Usually it is one of the narrowest of the weeping cherries in silhouette, with rather stiff branches. As it matures, larger limbs occasionally begin to mound upwards, so that the tree threatens to outgrow its site and, if this happens, pruning should be carried out before the culprit branches have a chance to become too big. They should be cut hard back to the stem, or to their parent limb, and the job should preferably be done in July or August.

P. a. Pendula is as floriferous as the wild upright form, the flowers appearing at the end of April or early in May, within a week or two of *P.* Hisakura. This Japanese cherry is also very free-flowering, but in deep pink, and the young leaves have an attractive coppery tinge as they open, framing the blossom delightfully. Hisakura is one of the smallest fan-shaped cherries, but the name is sometimes wrongly given to specimens of the more commonly planted variety Kanzan, which is considerably larger and heavier (see Plan 14.). Hisakura is easily distinguished by its single flowers, for those of the true Kanzan are heavily double.

The conifer of the group, *Cupressus glabra* Pyramidalis, is a variety of the smooth Arizona cypress which has a natural range in the USA from central Arizona to northern Mexico—a dry-lands background which ensures that it will flourish in soils which many trees would find too arid. It is one of the most picturesque of conifers, with red, peeling bark bright in contrast against the dense blue foliage and, since its introduction to Britain between the World Wars, it has become very popular as a garden conifer. Its formal shape and the intense blue of its foliage contrast with the white and pink mass of the single cherry blossom to perfection. It is an interesting tree for planting as a solitary specimen near the house, too, fascinating in the winter when the feathery sprays become peppered with tiny yellow flowers.

A quickly spreading ground-cover plant to front the group and carry it through the quiet summer period is the foam flower, *Tiarella cordifolia purpurea*, which has bronzy purple leaves, and produces clouds of starry pink flowers early in the summer.

If the rear of the group is in full, sunny view, so that the blue cypress has pride of place, a yellow-foliaged carpeting plant can provide a vivid contrast. There are several heathers which will do this,

44

The Chinese spring-flowering *Buddleia alternifolia* can be grown either as a large shrub or a gracefully arching standard tree

or the golden lemon-scented thyme, *Thymus* × *citriodorus* Aureus.

A colourful succession

From left to right: *Buddleia alternifolia*
                       Malus trilobata
                       Prunus Ito-kukuri

These are trees which will thrive in all types of soil, but none of them will stand overshading, as this will inhibit free flowering and cause them to lose their symmetry.

Buddleia alternifolia is often classed as a large shrub, but, with a little encouragement, it can be grown as a standard tree. Basal shoots should be restricted to one clean stem, and this must be tied to a firm stake and trained upright. When this is done, it makes one of the most beautiful of all small trees, with its gracefully arching, almost fully weeping habit, and narrow, dark green leaves, the branches wreathed

45

in June with fragrant purple blossom. It is good for this Chinese buddleia to be able to perform without competition at flowering time and, in this group, the flowering occurs in sequence, starting in April with the Japanese flowering cherry *Prunus* Ito-kukuri, which has semi-double flowers of the palest pink, followed by the southern European crabapple *Malus trilobata*, with white flowers opening in May, and culminating in the display from *Buddleia alternifolia.*

The stiffly erect Ito-kukuri and the neatly pyramidal *Malus trilobata* form a powerful contrast in silhouette seen against the informally arching buddleia. The contrast is seen also in the distinctive foliage: the pointed, willow-like leaves of the buddleia, the large, rounded cherry leaves with their bronzy tinge in the spring, colouring again before they fall, and the lobed maple-like leaves of the crabapple, which turn amber and orange in the autumn. This group must qualify as one of the most ornamental throughout the growing season.

Pruning in the case of the two upright trees will be limited to removing the occasional rogue branch at the most, but careful attention should be paid to this operation where *Buddleia alternifolia* is concerned, and it needs to be done every year. As soon as the flowers have faded—or by the end of July at the latest—all the shoots which have flowered should be cut off, leaving the new, arching growths intact to bear the following year's display. A tree which threatens to become too bulky for its site can have a large branch removed completely from the top of the stem, but this should not be done too often, or many potential flowers will be lost. The more familiar *B. davidii* is normally cut hard back in the spring, but *B. alternifolia* should never be treated in this way, or it will not flower.

The beautiful blossom, the pattern of crown shapes, and the varying leaf texture, all combine to ensure a continuity of interest until the autumn foliage colours appear, but some bright flower colour near ground level will flatter the trees during the late summer. Flame-coloured dahlias, for instance, especially the large flowered cactus type, if planted in front of the group, will bring out the russet tints which sometimes appear prematurely between the leaf veins at this season, and the warm reddish browns of the bark.

A crabapple group

From left to right: *Malus* Exzellenz Thiel

Malus yunnanensis veitchii

Malus Lady Northcliffe

This spring flowering selection will grow in any type of soil in an open, sunny garden.

The first to flower in this group is the hybrid weeping crabapple *Malus* Exzellenz Thiel, whose buds in April are bright pink, the petals opening to a very pale pink which fades as the flowers develop until it is pure white. In succession, the Chinese crab *M. yunnanensis veitchii* opens its white blossom, followed by Lady Northcliffe, bright pink in bud, the flowers again opening pure white. The three trees between them carry the flowering season through from April well into May.

During the late summer and autumn, there is a bonus of colour in the form of crabapple fruits: on Lady Northcliffe these are yellow; on *M. y. veitchii*, bright red; on Exzellenz Thiel they are a dull amber. These are really no more than berries, and cannot be used as culinary apples, but they are attractive on the tree. The foliage often colours brightly in the autumn, particularly the lobed leaves of *M. y. veitchii*, which turn orange and scarlet.

By habit, these are neat, if somewhat shrubby little trees, and they will usually keep within their expected crown silhouettes. If they should become straggly, wayward branches can be removed without difficulty, and the best time to do this occasional pruning is early June, after the flowers have faded.

A good herbaceous plant that will associate well with this group, and can be allowed to run freely up to their stems, is the creeping knotgrass *Polygonum affine* in one of its varieties, such as Darjeeling Red or Lowndes Variety. These are in flower from July to October, their numerous flower spikes changing from bright pink to ruby red as the autumn approaches. They add interest during the winter by retaining a cover of dry, brown leaves which help to keep the soil warm and weed-free.

A spring flowering and berrying group

From left to right: *Malus sieboldii*

       Sorbus Jermyns

       Prunus Yokihi

These ornamental trees are perfectly hardy, and will grow in almost any type of soil except those which are strongly alkaline, but they need full sunshine to do their best. An open, hillside situation will suit them well.

Malus sieboldii is a rather shrubby little crabapple from Japan, introduced to the West early in Queen Victoria's reign, and valued then as now for its elegant shape, its clustered blossom, pink in the bud opening to white, and the little red berry-like fruits that follow.

Sorbus Jermyns is the result of a cross between the British rowan and the Chinese mountain ash *S. sargentiana*. It flowers in May with large clusters of individually small white flowers, opening its buds as the crabapple blossom is fading. Later in the year it produces quite spectacular bunches of deep orange berries which last on the tree well after the leaves have fallen for the winter. Autumn is a colourful season for the group, for the leaves of all three trees take on glorious tints before they fall. Jermyns is not without interest during the winter, either, for its large dormant buds are red and sticky, and decorate the tall, neatly columnar form conspicuously.

The Japanese flowering cherry of the group, *Prunus* Yokihi, is one of the latest of its kind to come into flower, its pale pink blossom not opening until May so that, between the three trees, late spring is an exciting season. But this cherry is attractive in the early spring, too, before the semi-double blossom appears, for its young leaves have a strong bronzy tinge as they are expanding.

If this group is given the prominent sunny position it deserves, any supporting vegetation should continue the warm summer theme at ground level. It might be fronted, for instance, with a drift of dwarf lavender—such as the deep purple summer-flowering form Munstead Dwarf—which will always stay neatly in proportion to these small trees. When the lavender is planted on their sunny side, the fine foliage and fragrant flowers in mellow grey and purple will harmonise well with the tree foliage—the variously shaped dark green, lobed leaves of the crab, the small light green leaflets of the rowan, and the robust, dark leaves of the cherry.

A group for winter colour

From left to right: *Prunus cerasifera* Nigra
Chamaecyparis lawsoniana Winston Churchill
Salix alba Chermesina

Any reasonable garden soil will support this group, one of the most colourful selections, not only in the depth of winter but throughout the entire year. An open site is necessary, preferably a spot that will catch any sunshine that appears during the winter months. The cypress Winston Churchill must retain its foliage down to ground level.

A variety of the Middle Eastern myrobalan, *Prunus cerasifera* Nigra is not a weeping tree, although in silhouette it adopts a similarly graceful, curving habit. A purple-leaved plum—though plum fruits are very rarely produced—much of its great charm lies in the colour of its twigs and foliage, which are so dark a purple as to appear almost black. The young leaves are crimson after they open in the spring, darkening as they mature. The blossom in late March and early April is not spectacular but delicately beautiful, wreathing the branches with carmine as the buds are opening, soon fading to the palest pink blush as the petals expand.

Introduced at the close of World War II, Winston Churchill is one of the most distinguished Lawson's cypress varieties, with its neat, stocky outline, its sturdy, solidly dense leaf texture, and bright golden-yellow foliage that keeps its colour evenly during both summer and winter. The colour has an amber tinge that makes it ideal for placing between dark purple and bright red.

The wild white willow, *Salix alba*, a native of river banks in Great Britain, Europe and Asia, and a beautiful tree in its own right, is not for the small garden. While eminently suitable for damp and sandy places, it will grow virtually anywhere, including dry sites, but its roots under these circumstances will seek moisture so avidly that they may cause shrinkage of the clay beneath building foundations. The two coloured bark varieties, Chermesina and Vitellina, make sizeable trees, slightly less vigorous than the wild type, but, for small garden use, they can be grown in a very specialised way which ensures that they keep within reasonable limits. Willows have the ability to withstand frequent hard pruning—pollarding or coppicing—and they send out vigorous new shoots after this treatment, shoots which, having fresh young bark, are always the brightest in colour. The willow tree in this group should be cut hard back to the stump every second year in March. If a smaller tree is needed, it can be coppiced every year; if a taller tree is required, it can be grown as a single-stemmed standard to whatever branching height is needed, and cut back to that point.

For this arrangement, the scarlet-barked variety Chermesina is placed to match the dark purple plum, and to bring out the deep golden amber of the conifer—a purple and gold theme that will be intensified if there is some kind of dark background to frame the group in high relief whenever the winter sun shines.

There are many carpeting plants which will provide evergreen cover or a touch of colour at ground level; few that will fill the garden with fragrance during the coldest months. One such plant that will

A young, multi-stemmed specimen of the Chinese witch hazel, *Hamamelis mollis*, in flower during the winter months

associate happily with this group, and continue the winter garden theme below the trees, is the spreading evergreen *Sarcococca confusa*, which forms a year-round cover of dark, glossy green leaves, with deliciously fragrant creamy white flowers that open around Christmas time. This timing, and the appearance of its foliage have suggested the popular name for this shrub—Christmas box.

A winter and spring flowering group

From left to right: *Laburnum alpinum* Pendulum
Robinia pseudoacacia Pyramidalis
Hamamelis mollis

This is a hardy group that appreciates a reasonably sunny spot, and does well in any average garden soil—the most vigorous growth seems to be in sandy soils.

The strange, ribbon-like petals of the witch hazel flowers fill the air round about with their sweet perfume, wreathing the bare branches during the coldest months of the year, impervious to frost, ice or snow. The Chinese species *Hamamelis mollis* typically has bright yellow flowers—other witch hazels range in flower colour from pale lemon yellow to bright orange—which are on display from December

(Opposite) Salix alba Chermesina. For winter colour, the scarlet-barked willow should be cut back to the stump in the March of every second year

51

Robinia pseudoacacia Pyramidalis

to March, and usually at their best during January and February. Often, if left to its own devices, the downy-twigged *H. mollis*, with its wide-spreading habit, will grow into a tall, multi-stemmed shrub, but it can easily be trained to develop a single trunk, and the eventual overall height will be approximately the same in either case. The large, rounded, elm-like leaves, a soft downy green during the summer, turn bright yellow in the autumn.

Spring flowers are provided by two trees of the pea family—the upright robinia and the weeping Scotch laburnum. The false acacia, *Robinia pseudoacacia*, a native of the eastern USA, has been widely introduced to other parts of the world, and it often settles so readily that it has become naturalised in parts of Europe, and seeds itself freely in Britain. It is sometimes used for planting in industrial areas and near busy highways because of its high degree of resistance to smoke, grime and exhaust fumes. The upright form Pyramidalis lacks the fierce thorns that usually protect the species, so that it is easier to handle and, though it may eventually exceed the height planned for this group, its narrow outline will ensure that it does not outgrow a small garden. The delicate, fresh light green foliage is beautiful throughout the summer, contrasting strikingly with the dark, rugged bark, and the tree produces long, drooping clusters of white flowers in June, timed to correspond with the late-flowering *Laburnum alpinum* Pendulum. This variety of the so-called Scotch laburnum, which in fact originated in southern Europe, is another tree with fairly dainty, light green foliage. Its strongly weeping branches carry long clusters of golden chain flowers, appearing usually a fortnight later than those of the common laburnum.

The deciduous winter-flowering *Rhododendron mucronulatum* adds to the beauty of the winter scene, but is rather tall and rangy to qualify for a place of its own in a small garden, though it makes a charming companion for many small, open-crowned trees. It corresponds in its flowering season with the witch hazel and, beneath the spreading branches, its mauve flowers will stress the deep yellow of the *Hamamelis*. Around the rhododendron and beneath the other trees, a mass planting of sweet violets could be made, as they will establish a colony eagerly in these circumstances and, always welcome for the charm of their early spring flowers, will make a fresh, dark green carpet throughout the summer.

Plan 4
Groups of four, spreading to a total width of 8m (26ft)

An arrangement which will look equally presentable from the rear view; excellent as a screen between the garden and neighbouring land or a road, without seeming to have a screen's intent. It will never draw attention, as tall hedges will, to what it is intended to conceal. The actual area required on the ground measures 5m (16ft) by 3m (10ft)

Maples and conifers

From left to right: *Pinus cembra*
       Acer rubrum Scanlon
       Taxus baccata Fastigiata
       Acer palmatum Dissectum Flavescens
The trees in this group are happiest in a lime-free soil and a moderately sheltered situation. They have no objection to tall side shade, provided they are able to feel some sunlight. The Irish yew should not be stem pruned.

The tall column in this selection is provided by a variety of *Acer*

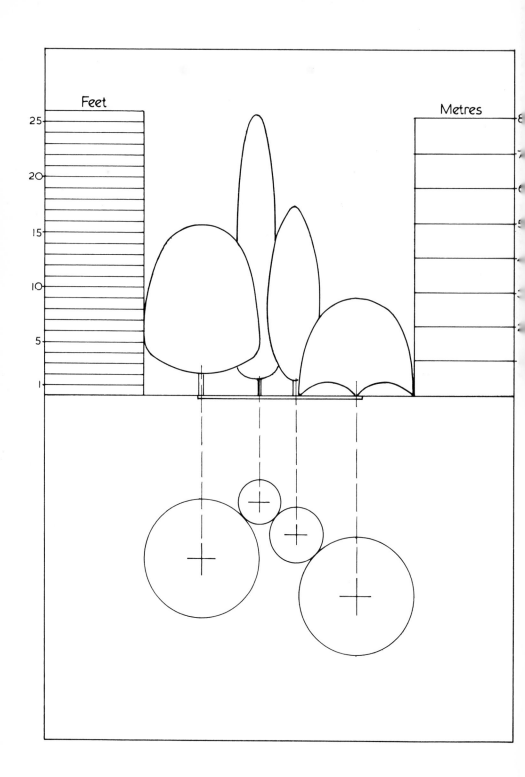

Feet

Metres

All the forms of *Acer palmatum* Dissectum, the cut-leaved maples, have a spreading, slowly mounding habit

rubrum, the red maple, named for the brilliance of its autumn leaf coloration and for its attractive reddish spring flowers. It is also known as the Canadian or swamp maple in North America, where it occurs as a wild tree not only in Canada, but over a vast natural range from Newfoundland to Florida, and from Dakota to Texas. Understandably, it will succeed in a wide variety of soils and sites but, as a rule, it grows slowly, especially when planted in limy soil. The clone Scanlon has all the features of the typical species, but it confines itself to this closely columnar silhouette.

The rounded, or semi-weeping member of the group is a cut-leaved variety of *A. palmatum*, usually called the Japanese maple, although it is found in China and Korea as well as Japan. A very variable plant, it is frequently seen as a small tree, though quite often it remains frankly a shrub—of the many named varieties, some are more shrubby than others. Dissectum Flavescens is noted for its spreading and mounding

Plan 4—Groups of four trees, spreading to a total width of 8m (26ft)

Taxus baccata Fastigiata

habit of growth and is one of the most ornamental forms of the species, with very deeply cut leaves of a warm yellow, especially bright in the spring, darkening to green for high summer. Despite the delicate appearance of its foliage, this maple is hardy over a surprisingly wide range, provided it is given the reasonably sheltered site and moderately fertile soil that will ensure healthy, steady growth.

The two maples are well balanced by the conifers in this group, with their well disciplined silhouettes. The Arolla pine, *Pinus cembra*, is at home in the mountains of central Europe and western Asia, where winters are notoriously long and hard. Under natural conditions, it makes a sizeable timber tree but, in the temperate zones of the USA and in Britain, where it has been grown as a garden tree since the mid eighteenth century, it puts on height very slowly, and seldom outgrows the limits of this design, forming a densely compact, symmetrical cone of stiff, dark green needles.

The Irish yew, *Taxus baccata* Fastigiata, is not found regularly in the wild. It was originally discovered as a wild seedling of the common yew in Ireland during the eighteenth century and, propagated vegetatively, it soon became popular, because of its sombre colour and dignified habit, for planting in churchyards. For the first few years after planting, it forms a narrow, rather straggly column, not developing the familiar solid shape until it is firmly established. Yews will grow even when they are heavily shaded, but this upright Irish form should never be completely overshadowed in this way or, remaining gappy and rangy, it will fail to thicken out to its firm textured fullness. The dark green, almost black shade of the yew's evergreen foliage is a wonderful foil for the colours and shapes of the maple leaves.

This contrast with the maples—their glorious autumn colours, the attractive bark that is so noticeable during the winter months, and the fascinating winged seeds that appear in clusters during the summer—makes this group one of the most telling selections, wherever a garish appearance needs to be avoided.

Dwarf shrubs that will associate happily with these trees include the varieties of *Potentilla fruticosa*: in the sunniest spots, the spreading, primrose yellow Elizabeth, and a taller clump of the bright yellow upright Jackman's Variety; in the shadier places, the orange-scarlet Sunset, and Tangerine with its orange flowers, or a clump of the bright scarlet Red Ace. Few plants have a longer summer flowering period than these shrubby potentillas, and their weed-excluding, sage-green foliage will always look right as a ground cover.

57

Crataegus laevigata Rosea Flore Pleno

A spring flowering group

From left to right: *Crataegus laevigata* Rosea Flore Pleno
                        Prunus Amanogawa
                        Juniperus virginiana Skyrocket
                        Prunus Kiku-shidare Sakura

This group needs a sunny site, but will succeed in all types of garden soil, acid or alkaline. The two upright trees, Amanogawa and Skyrocket, are extremely narrow and will not make a solid screen. Neither of them should be stem pruned in any way.

First to flower in March is the weeping cherry, Kiku-shidare Sakura, sweeping the ground with its glorious double pink flowers, followed in April by the equally floriferous, pale pink Amanogawa, with its startlingly contrasting shape. The double pink hawthorn, *Crataegus laevigata* Rosea Flore Pleno follows; in warm districts the blossom opens in May, but, in colder areas, the buds remain prudently closed until nearly June.

C. laevigata, the small hawthorn from Britain and the European

58

continent, has given rise to several beautiful garden forms. The wild species itself is very handsome and one of the most floriferous of the genus, often becoming completely covered with white or pale pink flowers. The berries that develop are very striking and, like those of the larger *C. monogyna*—the commoner of the two wild British hawthorns—they provide a reliable food supply for many kinds of birds in the autumn and early winter.

Skyrocket is a remarkably narrow little spire with probably the slimmest silhouette of any tree. It originated as a wild seedling of the pencil cedar, *Juniperus virginiana*, a juniper which is not confined to Virginia as its specific name might suggest, but is found over much of the east and central USA and as far north as Canada. The species is perfectly hardy in Britain, where it has been planted as a garden tree since the eighteenth century, but Skyrocket itself has been in commercial production only since World War II. It is very useful in the rock garden where its fine, silvery blue-grey foliage, with its closely compact texture, associates well with heathers and with the prostrate, spreading junipers. In this arrangement, it forms a double spire with the cherry Amanogawa—its equivalent among the extremely columnar hardwood trees. Amanogawa is one of the so-called Japanese cherries, said to have originated as a sport of the ancient Chinese hill cherry, *Prunus serrulata*. In recent years, it has become one of the best known flowering trees suitable for the tiniest garden, though it is not new and has been winning awards since as long ago as 1931.

Prunus Kiku-shidare Sakura is a very similar tree to Cheal's Weeping Cherry, which featured in Plan 1, and the two types have become inextricably confused by many growers. A plant by either name would give equally good results in this group. The juxtaposition of a weeping branch framework with the upright Amanogawa, and the foliage textures of the cherries in contrast with the hawthorn and the evergreen juniper, make this one of the most dramatic small tree groups.

The range of leaf texture and the pink spring blossom can be further accentuated by adding grey, sun-loving plants on the southern side of the arrangement. *Senecio greyi*—the rather untidy yellow daisy flowers can be clipped off in the bud—fronted by the much smaller *Santolina chamaecyparissus* and the carpeting *Stachys lanata* Silver Carpet, would be perfect for this purpose.

(Left) Juniperus virginiana Skyrocket, with probably the slimmest silhouette of any conifer, associates well with low, spreading shrubs

(Right) Prunus Kiku-shidare Sakura. A young specimen of this weeping cherry in a typical suburban setting

A graceful combination

From left to right: *Syringa vulgaris* Charles Joly
Laburnum anagyroides Erect
Clethra barbinervis
Prunus × *yedoensis* Shidare Yoshino

The trees in this group will grow well in most situations, but they appreciate a sunny site with a fairly moist and slightly acid soil, and some side shelter to break the worst of the winter's weather.

Charles Joly is a late-flowering variety of lilac, and its heavy, sweetly scented clusters of double purple flowers usually appear at the same time as those of the laburnum. *Syringa vulgaris* is an easily grown plant, but it has a tendency to adopt a shrubby instead of a tree-like habit; stems should be restricted to one, and any suckers which appear around the roots should be removed.

Erect is a strictly upright variety of the well known *Laburnum anagyroides* and originated as a seedling in Hillier's famous English nursery. It is a light-foliaged little tree which produces its spectacular golden chain flowers in the late spring. In its typical form, laburnum is a native of central and southern Europe, and thrives in those many parts of the world to which it has been introduced, seeding itself so freely that it has become naturalised in Britain and the United States.

60

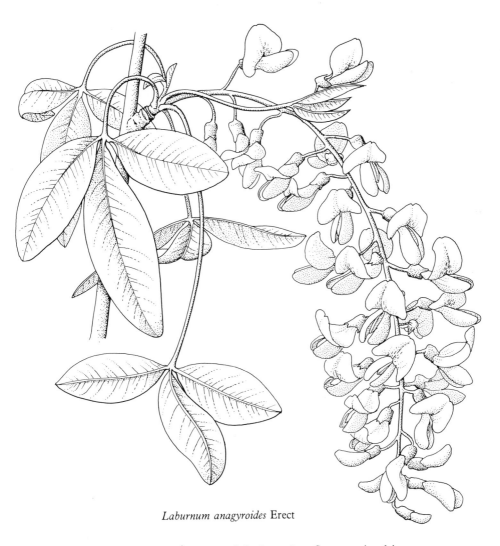

Laburnum anagyroides Erect

Clethra barbinervis also has graceful, drooping flowers, in this case white and sweetly fragrant, on display from July to September. This is a Japanese tree of neatly ovate outline, closely related to the American sweet pepper bush. The clustered, pointed leaves take on brilliant red and yellow autumn colours, especially in those years which experience an early frost.

The fourth tree is *Prunus* × *yedoensis* Shidare Yoshino, an almost fully weeping variety of the Japanese Yoshino cherry, and this produces its faintly fragrant pale pink flowers towards the end of March, opening the flowering season for the group long before the first leaves appear.

The refined harmony of this group is best not disrupted by too garish a colour combination at ground level; a pastel shade should be chosen and adhered to consistently at any one time, although, of course, the colour may well change in sequence with the seasons. Primroses look beautiful at the foot of the trees, and so do yellow-flowered bedding plants—perhaps a pale yellow strain of Coltness dahlias treated as annuals, if there is enough sun for them. If there is not enough light at ground level for low bedders such as these, ground-covering shrubs could be used. The central space in the arrangement could be occupied by *Mahonia japonica*, and the surrounding area by the low, spreading *M. aquifolium*. These handsome evergreens will carry the flowering season on so that colour is to be seen during every month of the year.

A distinguished choice

From left to right: *Magnolia* × *loebneri* Leonard Messel
Chamaecyparis lawsoniana Kilmacurragh
Malus Van Eseltine
Morus alba Pendula

Most normal garden conditions will support the trees in this group. Very shallow soils overlying chalk are not suitable, and the trees will grow best if the soil is peaty and moist and the site sheltered and reasonably warm. The conifer in this selection should not be stem pruned, but encouraged to retain its foliage to ground level.

This is a group of striking foliage and impressively sculptural outline, with a bonus of glorious spring and early summer flowers. The curtain-like branch structure of the weeping white mulberry, with its huge heart-shaped leaves—the traditional fodder for silkworm larvae—provides solidity for the pattern of contrasting silhouettes. The natural home of *Morus alba* is China, though it has for many centuries been cultivated in other parts of Asia and southern Europe for silk production. The berries are a pale pink, up to 2.5cm (1in) long, sweet, but rather tasteless. The flowers are inconspicuous, and the whole value of the weeping variety Pendula lies in its striking shape and the solidity of its texture. Though a good, fertile soil is needed for the full-sized, foliage-producing species, this variety does not need to achieve lush growth to develop its handsome outline, and it is happy in ordinary garden conditions.

The crabapple *Malus* Van Eseltine, with its distinctively upright stance, is one of the most beautiful of crabs when in blossom during

June. Its many-petalled flowers, each about 5cm (2in) across, strawberry red in the bud, opening pale pink, are followed later in the year by little yellow apples. A very hardy tree, it will succeed in any sunny site.

The variety of Lawson's cypress known as Kilmacurragh will also grow in any soil type, and forms a quite spectacular green column, so narrow and firm that it resists the snow damage to which many Lawson's varieties are prone. Though it may grow in height beyond the intentions of this plan, it will never become too broad for a small garden.

The magnolia comes into flower in April as its leaves are opening. The hybrid *Magnolia* × *loebneri* is one of the freest flowering magnolias, and its variety Leonard Messel is quite spectacular—even young plants become well covered with fragrant, narrow-petalled flowers of a deep mauve pink, a colour that is set perfectly against the opening buds of the crab and the tall green spire of Kilmacurragh. Magnolias usually prefer a moist, peaty soil, but Leonard Messel is one of the most tolerant of poor, limy conditions. The glorious flowers will last longer if the site is reasonably sheltered, but this variety will seldom disappoint its owner in the spring.

Those summer-flowering bedding plants or ground-covering shrubs which have a predominantly grey and purple colour might well be used to front this group, for plants of this hue will stress the strong but quiet foliage tones of the trees. The lavenders will do this, and so will the hybrid catmint *Nepeta* × *faassenii*, with its silvery grey leaves and pale purple flowers throughout the summer months.

Plan 5
Groups of four, spreading to a total width of 9m (30ft)

This is a compact arrangement that might be allowed to back directly against a boundary fence, so that the branches of the two columnar trees are overhanging the adjoining land. The actual area on the ground measures 6.25m (21ft) by 2.75cm (9ft).

A maple grove

From left to right: *Acer platanoides* Globosum
Acer saccharum Temple's Upright
Acer japonicum
Acer cappadocicum

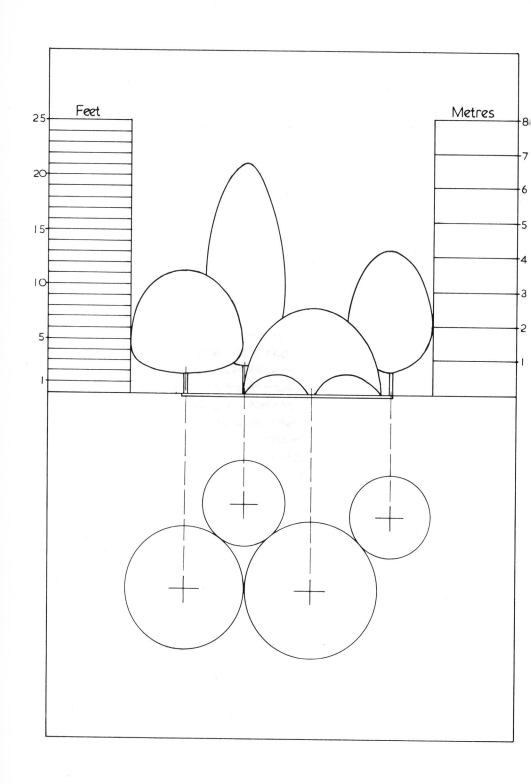

Feet

Metres

25
20
15
10
5
1

8
7
6
5
4
3
2
1

Acer platanoides Globosum

For this group of maples, two from the Old World and two from the New, a rather sheltered site is preferable, not because they are tender, but because cold winds can damage the young leaves. They will grow in any reasonable soil, but their famous autumn colours are brighter in acid ones.

The typical Norway maple is not to be planted in small gardens, for it makes a large and vigorous tree that will soon outgrow the site. The variety *Acer platanoides* Globosum, though fairly large specimens are to be found, takes many years to exceed the bounds of the average small plot. Its closely compact, globose crown bears full-sized 15cm (6in) five-lobed leaves, of a fine dark green which usually turns bright yellow in the autumn.

A. saccharum the sugar maple is valued as a timber producer in North America, where its natural range lies within the vast area bounded by Newfoundland, South Dakota, Texas and South Carolina, and it has also been planted very widely elsewhere as an ornamental tree. The very beautiful 15cm (6in) lobed leaves, rather similar to those of the Norway maple, turn bright orange and crimson most autumns. The typical species has never grown well enough in Britain to be planted extensively, but the variety Temple's Upright seems to like the climate, perhaps because it has a natural tendency to grow

Plan 5—Groups of four trees, spreading to a total width of 9m (30ft)

more slowly than the species, and its narrowly upright stance fits it admirably for garden use.

The Japanese maple *A. japonicum* is one of the most variable of trees but, on average, it has the rounded, pendant-twigged habit that will fit the silhouette in this arrangement. There are numerous beautiful varieties from which to choose, all with attractive foliage; the typical species has soft green leaves which colour red and yellow in the autumn, but there are cultivars with yellow leaves, others with their foliage red or purple throughout the growing season, and several with differing degrees of leaf lobing—some of almost fern-like fineness. Two distinct varieties are listed in Plans 7 and 9.

A. cappadocicum is a handsome maple from the drier regions of central Asia where, in its native hills, it will attain 20m (65ft) or more. Under garden conditions it will rarely exceed a useful 6m (20ft) and grows well in most soil types, producing a characteristically beehive-shaped crown. Autumn sees the broad, glossy leaves turning a clear yellow, but there are several excellent varieties which have coloured leaves throughout the summer, especially Rubrum with red leaves and Aureum with yellow.

Maples such as these have an extra attraction in their ornamental winged seeds which appear in clusters during the late summer, and the flowering season does not pass unnoticed either. They all produce attractive spring flowers, and those of *A. platanoides* in yellow, and *A. japonicum* in red, are particularly conspicuous.

For a soil that is on the acid side, nothing looks better growing around the feet of these trees than one of the North American creeping evergreen shrubs, such as *Gaultheria procumbens*, which makes a neat carpet of glossy, dark green, scented leaves. The small flowers in the late summer are white or pink, and the bare winter months are lent interest by the bright red 'partridge berries' which often remain to decorate the smart evergreen cover.

Some shapely berrying trees

From left to right: *Malus* Almey
                     Sorbus Signalman
                     Malus Red Jade
                     Diospyros lotus

A sunny site in any garden soil will support these trees, which will draw attention with their charms throughout the growing season, and present a pleasing silhouette during the winter months.

In late April and early May, the two crabapples in this group between them produce a profusion of pink and white blossom. The two-tone flowers of *Malus* Almey, with their strawberry red petals and white centres, appear pink from a slight distance, and *Malus* Red Jade—one of the most beautiful of weeping trees—also has pink and white blossom. Red Jade is a little tree which could well be planted to stand alone on a sunny mound, so that its elegant shape could be admired without distraction, but it also takes its place with grace, as here, in a group. Later in the season, the berry-like apples of Red Jade are cherry red, those of Almey bright orange; in both cases, they persist on the branches long after the leaves have fallen and well into winter, bright enough to gleam in the frosty sunshine.

The hybrid *Sorbus* Signalman was the result of a cross between the European service tree and the dwarf mountain ash from America. It is a compact little tree able, like its parents, to flourish on dry, exposed sites as well as in normal garden conditions. The blossom has a somewhat off-white hue, but it corresponds in season with the two crabs, and helps to boost their charm. Its fine, small leaves are attractive throughout the summer and, in the autumn, the brilliant red clustered berries are outstanding. It was the brilliance of these massed berries so well displayed by the tree's upright stance that suggested the name Signalman to its raisers, Hilliers.

Diospyros lotus is known as the date plum and is closely related to the North American persimmon. A native of the Far East, it was introduced to Europe during the sixteenth century, and has proved perfectly hardy in Britain, where it thrives in all types of soil. It makes a shapely little tree with its dark green, glossy foliage, and female plants bear small, plum-like fruits in purple or yellow. It is a one-sex tree, so the plant must be female for fruit production, and there is no need to plant a male tree as well, to pollinate the female flowers, unless they are intended to produce fertile seed.

The berrying theme can be continued at ground level by planting the creeping evergreen shrub, *Viburnum davidii*, which builds low mounds of glossy dark green leaves. Though the white flowers in June are not very conspicuous, they result in bright blue fruits which persist among the green cover throughout the winter months. Like the date plum, *V. davidii* is usually a one-sex plant but, in this case, both sexes are needed for the berries to appear, so several specimens should be planted together in the first instance.

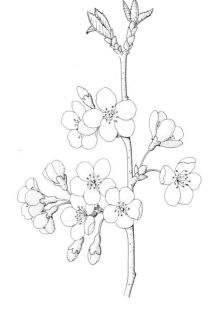

Prunus cerasifera Pissardii

Prunus × *hillieri* Spire

A **Prunus** *collection for spring display*

From left to right: *Prunus cerasifera* Pissardii
                          Prunus × *hillieri* Spire
                          Prunus Pink Shell
                          Prunus kurilensis Ruby

A selection noted for their hardiness and ability to thrive in poor soils, they will all grow in the shade of larger trees, but this will cause them to lose their compact shapes and produce only a poor show of flowers. To be seen at their best, they need an open, sunny site.

The myrobalan plum, *Prunus cerasifera*, originated in eastern Europe and western Asia, and the form Pissardii is said to have been first grown in the garden of the then Shah of Persia, during the reign of Queen Victoria. With its neat form, its prolific pale pink blossom during March and April, and its colourful stems and leaves—ranging from green and crimson to dark purple—it has become a very popular garden tree, widely planted in Europe, Britain and North America, where it has proved its extreme hardiness and tolerance by thriving in many an inclement situation. Its compact shape and quick response to clipping have led to its frequent use as a hedge plant, a function which it fulfils admirably.

68

P. × hillieri, the hybrid cherry of which the variety Spire is a selected form, has as its parents two highly acclaimed Japanese trees: the bush-like bonsai favourite Fuji cherry, *P. incisa*, and the vigorous round-headed *P. sargentii*. Spire itself is one of the most symmetrical of the flowering cherries, with its strictly upright form. It takes many years for a specimen to broaden in the crown to any extent—the original Spire, from which all the trees of this name have been cloned, is barely 3.75m (12ft) in breadth, and the average mature specimen spans no more than 3m (10ft).

Prunus Pink Shell is a Japanese flowering cherry of chance seedling origin. It is one of the most graceful of its kind, in appearance almost delicate, though it is as hardy as any. Its slender branches become wreathed during early April with single flowers of the palest pink.

P. kurilensis Ruby is also a very ornamental little tree, in shape and build rather like a stockier version of Amanogawa, with a more solid branch system, covered with pale pink blossom in April. When this blossom appears, the outer part of each expanding flower is a rich ruby red, giving the whole tree a glowing appearance while the leaf buds are starting to open. The species *P. kurilensis* is sometimes classified as a variety of the Japanese alpine cherry, *P. nipponica*.

These members of the genus *Prunus* are among the most distinguished spring flowerers, and the display of blossom during April—though over comparatively soon—is such a symphony in pink while it lasts, that any attempt to bolster the picture at this season, with added colour from adjacent plants, would be wasted. Their attraction does not end with April, of course, and the well-balanced symmetry of the group enhances the healthy green of the summer foliage, which changes to tawny orange and crimson in the autumn.

The pink theme could be carried through the summer, however, with pink flowered bedders in the sunny foreground—the annuals *Zinnia* Pink Ruffles and *Aster* Milady Rose, or a perennial plant such as *Sidalcea* Loveliness. If the area is too shady for these flowers, a permanent framework could be arranged of the red-leaved barberry, *Berberis thunbergii atropurpurea* and the dwarf Atropurpurea Nana.

An unusual group of contrasting beauty

From left to right: *Cercidiphyllum magnificum*
      Morus alba Pyramidalis
      Acer palmatum Dissectum Atropurpureum
      Taxus baccata Fastigiata Aurea

Morus alba Pyramidalis

These trees will do best in a sheltered garden where the soil is loamy and slightly acid and, although side shade is permissible, they must be able to feel sunlight on their crowns. The yew, being a conifer, will be clothed with foliage down to the ground, and the others of this group will also lend themselves very effectively to low branching and, with this end in mind, feathered trees can be planted instead of standards.

The beauty of this group depends almost entirely on foliage and shape. *Cercidiphyllum magnificum* has flowers which are small and inconspicuous, but the leaves are attractive and take on bright yellow tints in the autumn. It is rarely planted in gardens, being less well known than the larger *C. japonicum*. In its native Japan it makes an impressive tree, but when grown under garden conditions it is often little more than a large and shapely shrub.

The upright form of the white mulberry, *Morus alba* Pyramidalis, also has interesting foliage, and its amazingly fastigiate form, with its cover of huge heart-shaped leaves, forms a dramatic exclamation mark above this unusual group. As with the weeping white mulberry described under Plan 4, it can be used as fodder for silkworm larvae, but it would surely be unfeeling to rob this magnificent little tree of its leaves.

Dissectum is a name which covers a group of cultivated varieties of the Japanese maple *Acer palmatum*, all with deeply cut leaves and a spreading, semi-weeping, slowly mounding habit of growth. They display a range of foliage colour, and Dissectum Atropurpureum has many-lobed leaves of a deep purple, not just in the autumn, but throughout the summer months. This colourful Oriental tracery is greatly enhanced by the architectural solidity of the slenderly contrasting mulberry.

The golden Irish yew, *Taxus baccata* Fastigiata Aurea, also known as Fastigiata Aureomarginata, was first propagated towards the end of the nineteenth century, as a sport variegation of the dark green upright Irish yew. This beautiful columnar tree takes a few years to become well established after planting, but, eventually, it thickens itself into a firm, solid pillar of golden green which contrasts perfectly with the crimson-purple of the bushy-leaved maple immediately next to it.

These trees will look absolutely delightful beside a rocky pool, with ferns and low bulbs, or other non-obtrusive plants, beyond their branch spread.

Plan 6
Groups of four, spreading to a total width of 10m (33ft)

An arrangement of trees similar in outline to those in Plan 5, but on a larger scale. As before, they could be planted hard against a boundary wall so that the lowest branches of the upright trees can overhang the adjoining land. The actual area to be planted measures 6.75m (23ft) by 2.75m (9ft).

An unusual woodland garden group

From left to right: *Maackia chinensis*
Stewartia pseudocamellia
Fontanesia phillyreoides
Stewartia monodelpha

This striking group needs a lime-free woodland type of soil, with plenty of humus material to retain the moisture—peat is a welcome addition—and tall side shade, or light overhead shade.

These little trees are attractive throughout the year, with an unforgettable summer display of white flowers which show up the better for their shaded setting. *Maackia chinensis* has spikes of white pea-family flowers which appear in midsummer, and it is silvery-white in the leaf, too, as the foliage is expanding during the spring. A hardy little Chinese tree which has taken readily to a wide range of sites and climatic conditions away from its native habitat, it will do well as a garden specimen in most kinds of soil. It grows very slowly to its maximum height, and for many years the crown shape is rounded but, the main limbs being inclined upwards, encroaching age inevitably sees the branch pattern flatten, and the crown broaden to as much as 5m (16ft) across.

The stewartias are typical woodland garden trees, and they need the traditional woodland conditions: light shade and a lime-free, preferably peaty soil. Hardy in southern Britain and the milder areas of the USA, *Stewartia monodelpha* is a comparatively little known Japanese species which, though it may attain large tree size in its native woods, seldom exceeds 5m (16ft) in Western gardens. Its neat little spire becomes covered with magnificent white flowers over two full summer months, and it usually displays bright autumn tints before the leaves fall.

Also from Japan is the better known *Stewartia pseudocamellia*, a little

(Opposite) After a few years' growth, the golden Irish yew, *Taxus baccata* Fastigiata Aurea, makes a solid pillar of golden green

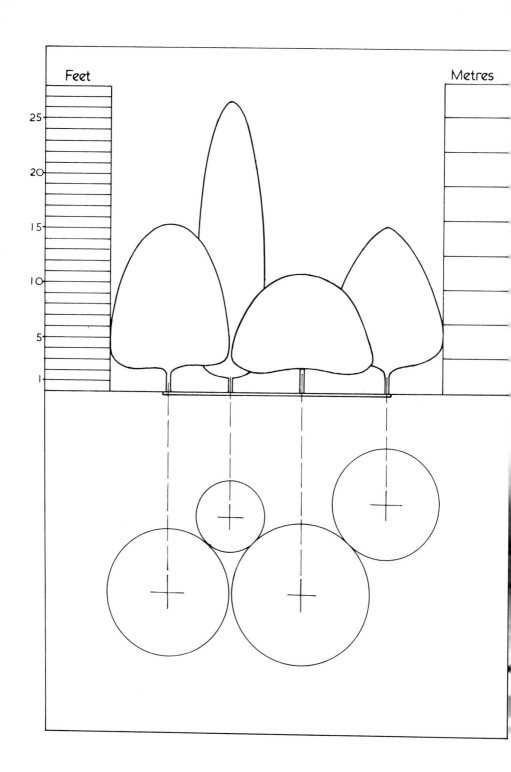

Feet

Metres

25

20

15

10

5

1

Maackia chinensis is a slow growing and very hardy little Chinese tree which needs a lime-free, woodland type of soil

hardier than *S. monodelpha*, so that it will thrive all over Britain and much of North America, provided it has the right conditions of soil and woodland side shade. After colouring brightly in scarlet and yellow shades before leaf fall, it is very handsome during the bare winter months, too, with its flaking, patchwork bark. Stewartias have a tendency to grow shrub-fashion, with several main stems, and these multi-stemmed trees eventually become more open and spreading than they would otherwise do. If garden space makes it important for them to retain the slim proportions of their youth, these leading stems should be restricted to one or two only, so that they can keep their very neat, columnar habit. The beautiful flowers in July and August,

Plan 6—Groups of four trees, spreading to a total width of 10m (33ft)

Stewartia pseudocamellia

5cm (2in) across the white cups, are reminiscent of a camellia.

Completely hardy, and eager to grow in the type of soil and sheltered site that the others of this group enjoy, *Fontanesia phillyreoides* is a native of Turkey, introduced to Britain some two centuries ago. It forms a very neat oval, with small dark green leaves and little creamy flowers during the summer. It is an interesting tree during the winter, too, with its rough, dark bark.

A woodland group like this will need small woodland plants to accompany it and complete the picture. A good evergreen ground-covering shrub of the right kind is the glossy-leaved bear grape, *Arctostaphylos uva-ursi*, which has pink flowers in the spring, followed by brilliant red berries.

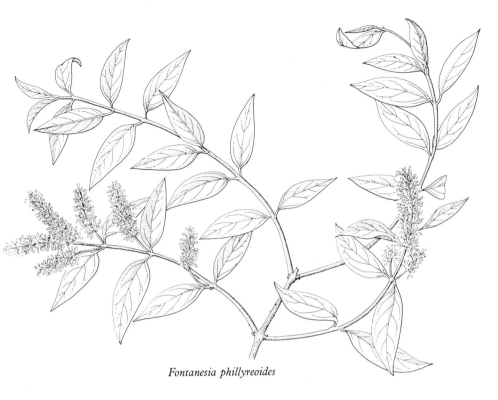

Fontanesia phillyreoides

A colourful group from spring to autumn

From left to right: *Sorbus vilmorinii*
                          Prunus Shosar
                          Prunus Shirotae
                          Syringa vulgaris Madame Lemoine

These trees will thrive in most soil types, even on poor or very exposed sites, but they all need the sun and must not be overshadowed. One-sided shade will produce imbalance in their branching systems, and can cause the lilac in particular to collapse.

A Chinese mountain ash that was introduced to the West a century back, *Sorbus vilmorinii* grows into a very ornamental little tree which produces a good show in May when laden with heavy clusters of white blossom, and again in the autumn when the tiny-leaved, almost fern-like foliage takes on warm tints and the branches are hung with loosely pendulous clusters of pale pink berries.

The two Japanese flowering cherries in this selection are perfectly matched both in form and in flower. *Prunus* Shosar is a vigorous little tree which bears its single pink flowers often as early as the last week

77

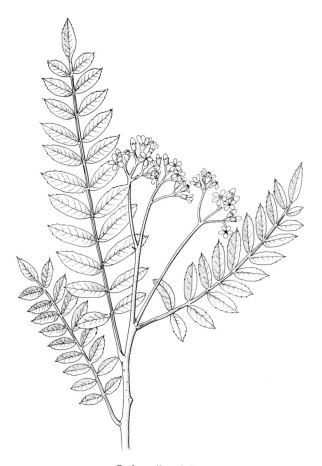

Sorbus vilmorinii

in March, with the bulk of its display in early April. *P.* Shirotae, following in quick succession, is equally vigorous in its different way, for this is a spreading tree which often adopts a weeping habit. The branch tips at any rate have a strong tendency to droop, especially when heavy with blossom, and it is one of the prettiest of the Japanese cherries in April, with its large, fragrant, semi-double white flowers in long, pendulous clusters. Both trees have bright green foliage which colours amber and russet in the autumn.

Any one of the many varieties of lilac, *Syringa vulgaris*, would take its place admirably in this group, though most of them are rather more

(Opposite) This vigorous little Japanese cherry, *Prunus* Shosar, often bears its single pink flowers before the end of March

Prunus Shirotae, drooping beneath the weight of its white flowers, is one of the prettiest of the Japanese cherries in April

rounded in silhouette than the plan shows. There are numerous named varieties, all similar in stature and ranging in flower colour from pure white through the traditional lilac shades to deep crimson. Pure pink lilacs are rare, so perhaps the deliciously fragrant Madame Lemoine, cream in the bud, opening to white, is the one that will best follow the cherries and carry the spring flowering theme through until early June. A newly planted lilac tree should be encouraged to form a sturdy single stem, at least to waist height, so that it takes on the characteristics of a small tree, rather than a large shrub.

A low, shrubby, evergreen cover which has bright colour during the mid and late summer period, such as *Hypericum calycinum*, known in England as the rose of Sharon, with its exuberant, bright yellow flowers, would be ideal if planted and allowed to spread around the stems and beyond the crowns of these little trees. Early spring bulbs such as chionodoxas can be planted among these ground-covering shrubs, and will display their sky blue flowers unhindered, if the shrubby growth is clipped back to near ground level every winter.

(Opposite) Cornus florida rubra, a wild variety of the North American flowering dogwood, is conspicuous in the spring with its pink bracts

80

A group with long-lasting ornamental fruits

From left to right: *Crataegus maximowiczii*
                      Sorbus Ethel's Gold
                      Malus Elise Rathke
                      Diospyros virginiana

The trees in this group will grow in any soil in a sunny garden.

Crataegus maximowiczii is a usually thornless hawthorn from Siberia, as hardy as any of the American or European species and able to thrive in garden conditions, but it needs sunlight to retain the very distinctive domed shape of its crown. It has unhawthorn-like rounded leaves, but produces a display of typical white may blossom early in June, while late summer and autumn sees the development of a good show of bright red berries which last on the tree as long as the birds spare them.

Sorbus Ethel's Gold arose by chance as a hybrid between two species of mountain ash. Following the clusters of typical white rowan flowers in May, it produces a wonderful display of golden-yellow berries in the autumn, and these persist on the leafless branches for much of the winter, as birds seem to find them less appetising than the more usual red rowan berries.

Malus Elise Rathke is a beautiful little weeping crabapple which, like the mountain ash Ethel's Gold, arose as a chance hybrid seedling from unknown parents. It has white flowers, appearing usually late in April, and these have the appearance of domestic apple blossom pinkish in the bud, but opening to pure white. Later in the year, it develops sweet and edible miniature yellow apples, so it is a useful as well as an ornamental little tree, which flowers and fruits best if given a sunny site.

Diospyros virginiana is the persimmon, a native of the southern USA, from Carolina to Mexico. In its natural habitat it can grow as tall as 15m (50ft), but in other parts of the world such as Britain—where it was introduced early in the seventeenth century—it seldom exceeds the dimensions assumed by this plan. It is not a particularly symmetrical tree in the shape of its crown, but it always looks neat and attractive, with its glossy green leaves that turn red and yellow in the autumn before falling to reveal picturesque bark that is patterned with deep furrows. Persimmon fruits, when they appear in late summer, look like red-cheeked yellow crabapples and measure

(Opposite) Wisteria floribunda Macrobotrys, a variety of the Japanese wisteria grown as a standard tree. The flower clusters can measure 1m (3ft 4in)

about 3cm (1¼in) across. It is a one-sex tree, so female plants are needed for a display of fruit, and these are produced without the need for pollination by male flowers, though they will not, of course, contain fertile seed.

The yellow, red and orange autumn theme of this fruiting group can be accented by the use of late flowering herbaceous plants such as dwarf Michaelmas daisies—the large-flowered, pale blue Audrey or the double violet-purple Jenny grow scarcely more than 30cm (12in) in height, and are in flower during October when the berries are at their colourful best.

A collection of small maples

From left to right: *Acer grandidentatum*
Acer macrophyllum Seattle Sentinel
Acer × coriaceum
Acer maximowiczii

Maples, in the main, are very hardy trees which will flourish in all reasonable types of soil. They have no objection to side shade, but enjoy a touch of sunlight on their crowns. The ornamental foliage keeps its healthy colour better in sites sheltered from cold winds.

Included in this group are two of the native North American maples which help to make the western mountainous regions a blaze of colour, red, orange and yellow, during the autumn. Though their brilliance at this season is legendary, they are beautiful trees throughout the year. The bigtooth maple, *Acer grandidentatum*, from the Rocky Mountains and northern Mexico, has three- or five-lobed, red-stemmed leaves and clusters of greenish-pink winged seeds. A slow-growing little tree when planted in Britain, it makes a good partner for *A. macrophyllum*, the bigleaf or Oregon maple. This is a native of the western coastal region of North America from Alaska to southern California, and the city of Seattle is virtually central to this range. Seattle Sentinel itself is a very fine columnar tree with handsome, glossy green leaves, up to 30cm (12in) long, with five deeply cut lobes. The flowers in April are sweetly scented in large, drooping clusters of sulphur yellow, followed by bunches of very pretty winged seeds.

A. × coriaceum, a hybrid between the European sycamore and the southern European Montpelier maple, also bears clusters of yellowish flowers in April, followed by bunches of keys. It grows into a neat little tree with glossy, three-lobed leaves which usually retain their conservative dark green shade in the autumn, to act as a foil to the brilliance of the others in the group. It has been grown as a garden tree for two hundred years or more, and has proved to be one of the hardiest of maple hybrids.

In the case of *A. maximowiczii*, a Chinese species, the three- or five-lobed leaves not only colour a bright crimson in the autumn, they also sport a tinge of red throughout the growing season. It is a handsome tree in the winter, too, with its beautifully striated bark.

Maples are among the prettiest of trees and, more than most, they suggest the woodland glade—the forest borders where rays of sunlight slant through the tree crowns, a habitat in which grass and herbs are able to grow without being overshadowed, and the contrast between light and shade is most pronounced. Something of this atmosphere can be captured if lawn grass is allowed to run freely, brushed by the skirts of the maples, their lower branches left unpruned, so that the picturesque foliage contrasts with neatly mown turf.

Plan 7
Groups of five, spreading to a total width of 11m (36ft)

This is a compact arrangement of individually quite bulky trees, which will tend to make the area of ground they occupy appear bigger than it actually is. The larger tree at the rear can be grown hard against a boundary wall but, in most of the groups, the small, shrubby trees at either end of the arrangement look better when clothed with foliage down to the ground. Actual planting area between stems is about 8.5m (28ft) by 3.75m (12ft).

A screening group for a sunny garden

From left to right: *Hibiscus syriacus*
Ginkgo biloba Pendula
Crataegus monogyna Stricta
Crataegus coccinioides
Euonymus semiexsertus

These trees prefer a warm, sunny, dryish site, and will grow in any type of garden soil.

Known in America as the rose of Sharon, the hardy mallow *Hibiscus syriacus* from the Middle East has been grown in Western gardens for hundreds of years, and there are many beautiful varieties, most of which are seen as multi-stemmed, domed shrubs. Some of them will

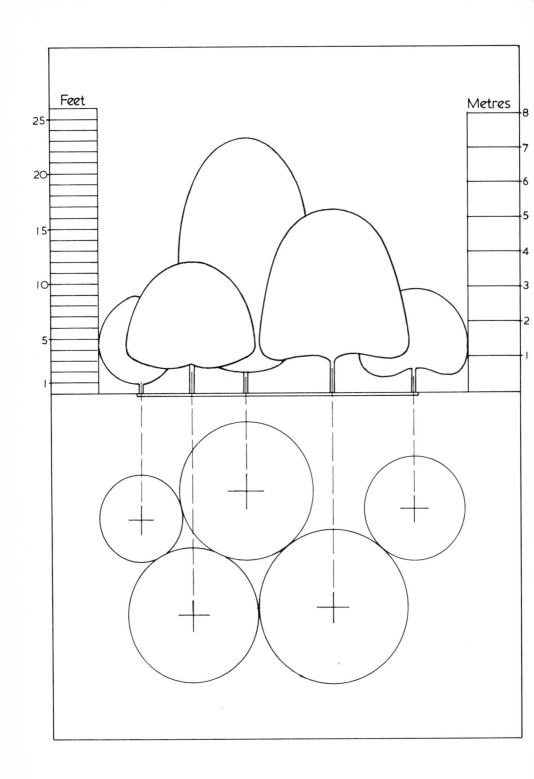

Feet

25 —
20 —
15 —
10 —
5 —
1 —

Metres

8
7
6
5
4
3
2
1

attain small tree proportions and can be grown as standards if they are encouraged from the start to develop a single stem and a definite crown of branches. A few of the most vigorous varieties suitable for training in this way are: Woodbridge, with single carmine flowers; Blue Bird, one of the most popular, with single violet flowers; and Ardens, which is naturally erect, and readily makes a small tree, with pale purple double flowers. The 5cm (2in) wide trumpet flowers are usually on display from late summer until autumn.

The weeping variety of the maidenhair, *Ginkgo biloba* Pendula, is a somewhat variable tree, as there are several weeping strains of the species, but they all form a slowly growing mound of closely arranged branches and contorted twigs, which eventually make an impervious barrier. Maidenhair is a strange tree—a conifer, with broad, fan-shaped leaves which turn yellow before falling in the autumn. It is sometimes called a 'living fossil', for it is the only surviving member of a primitive group of plants which once covered many parts of the world. The typical species is tall and straight, quite unlike the variety Pendula.

Two hawthorns, one from the Old World and one from the New, provide the thick, close foliage texture and high, domed shapes needed to form the bulk of this screen. *Crataegus monogyna* is the common British hedgerow quickthorn, which often paints the countryside white with blossom from May to June and decorates it with bright red berries in the autumn. The species has been introduced into North America, and is now semi-naturalised in many places. Stricta, the variety used in this selection, is an erect growing, fastigiate form, with a dense, twiggy, thorny crown, as handsome in blossom as the type, and very much appreciated in the early winter by the birds which feed on its clustered haws. *C. coccinioides* is a native of Canada and the eastern United States, often planted in American gardens, and this hawthorn, in its turn, has frequently been seen in British gardens too since its introduction towards the close of the nineteenth century. To frame the white spring blossom, the young foliage is charmingly tinged with red, becoming green for the summer, only to colour brightly again in the autumn as an accompaniment for the large dark crimson berries.

Euonymus semiexsertus is a Japanese spindle tree which was introduced to the West during the late nineteenth century, a neatly rounded bush with close, screen-making foliage, very pretty in the autumn when it produces conspicuous red and pink fruits.

Plan 7—Groups of five trees, spreading to a total width of 11m (36ft)

Crataegus monogyna Stricta

The trees in this group, with their intricate branch systems and closely arranged foliage, make a very efficient screen, particularly if they can be grown with their foliage intact and clothing the stems down to ground level. For this purpose, 'feathered' plants will have to be obtained rather than standard trees, which have already had their lowest branches removed by the nursery. On the warm, sunny sites that will suit the trees best, this low, spreading foliage could well be fronted with colourful flowers: a cottage garden mixture of annual bedders. Pruned trees, on the other hand, might be carpeted with the winter-flowering *Jasminum nudiflorum*, which will slowly mound up to give a feeling of solidity at the base of the group, besides providing a bonus of charming yellow flowers in mid winter.

An unusual spring flowering group

From left to right: *Halesia carolina*
                            Malus Kaido
                            Cornus nuttallii
                            Malus glaucescens
                            Prunus Taoyama Zakura

88

A reasonably sheltered site is best, with a rather acid soil that has not been limed. The trees have no objection to tall side shade, but they must not be overshadowed too heavily on one side, or they will lose their symmetry.

Out of the usual run of spring flowering trees, this group presents a restrained but beautiful show of white and pink blossom, lasting from about the last week in April to the end of May or early June. First to flower is *Prunus* Taoyama Zakura, a distinguished little Japanese cherry of bushy habit, growing and spreading slowly into its distinctive shape, with fragrant, semi-double, pale pink flowers which are garlanded so profusely as to hide the branches.

The snowdrop tree, *Halesia carolina*, from the south-eastern USA, grows to a larger size in its native habitat than specimens usually attain under garden conditions. It has been cultivated in Britain since the mid eighteenth century, and has received awards for the decorative qualities of the beautiful white bells which festoon its branches in May.

Two crabapples, one from the East and one from America, join forces very effectively with their similarly outlined but differently sized shapes. *Malus* Kaido is a hybrid between the pink flowered Chinese crabapple *M. spectabilis*, and the white flowered Siberian crab, *M. baccata*. Kaido produces masses of pink blossom in May and, as a specimen tree, is able to flourish in all types of soil, as hardy as any other of the apple family in Britain or the United States. It has a very neat, compact crown of branches that fits it admirably to a supporting role in a group such as this. *M. glaucescens*, a crabapple which is to be found growing wild in the eastern USA, has often been planted as a garden tree, both in America and England, where it was introduced early in the twentieth century. Its distinctively lobed leaves, dark green on the upper surface and grey beneath, display bright purple tints in the autumn. During May, the branches are covered with pink blossom, followed later in the year by little green apples. Occasionally, individual trees are found which are lacking a central stem so that they retain shrub-like proportions, but, usually, the species forms a distinctively crowned standard tree.

The group has another American species in *Cornus nuttallii*, the western dogwood, a native of the Pacific coastal area where, in the humid forest, it often grows to a narrow 10m (33ft)—a height it is unlikely to reach when planted in Britain or other areas. It is perfectly hardy in Britain, however, and has grown well since its introduction early in the nineteenth century. Like the snowdrop tree, it dislikes

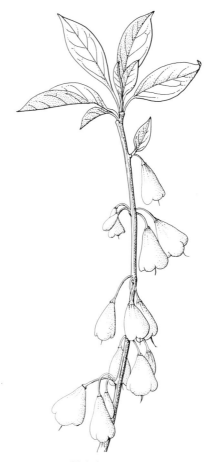

Halesia carolina

lime but, with this reservation, will thrive in any reasonably good soil. May sees the production of a grand show of 7.5cm (3in) bract flowers, with four, six or eight 'petals' in white or the palest blush pink, and the rounded leaves colour brightly before falling in the autumn. The variety of western dogwood known as North Star grows more vigorously than the typical species, but its crown shape is less symmetrical.

A shallow-rooting shrub that will slowly mound up around the stems, luxuriate in the semi-shade, keep the ground clean and free of weeds, and add a highlight of interest during the winter months, would surely benefit the group. One such evergreen is *Euonymus fortunei radicans* Variegatus, with brightly patterned leaves of silver and gold, tinged with green and pink.

For year-round beauty

From left to right: *Acer japonicum* Vitifolium
Malus Wintergold
Aesculus pavia
Prunus cerasus Semperflorens
Pyrus salicifolia Pendula

This group of trees will flourish in any sunny garden, and in soils ranging from acid to alkaline, sandy to clayish.

The contrast in foliage between members of this group is really quite striking. *Acer japonicum*, a Japanese maple, is one of the most varied of trees, with many different forms, all with beautiful foliage. The variety Vitifolium has broad, conspicuously lobed leaves, rather like those of a fig tree, soft green in the spring and summer, colouring gloriously crimson and orange in the autumn. The flowers in April are also pretty, in pendulous red clusters, conspicuous against the fresh sage-green of the unfurling leaves.

Next to flower is the small hybrid crabapple *Malus* Wintergold, which owes its name to the heavy crops of golden yellow apples which remain on the branches long after the leaves have fallen for the winter, and glow in the pale sunlight. The blossom is pink in the bud, but this colour is limited to the petal reverse, and the flowers open white.

Prunus cerasus Semperflorens is the All Saints cherry, which produces clusters of white flowers during May and from then onwards sporadically throughout the summer, when they appear here and there along the slightly weeping branches. All Saints cherry is a variety of the sour cherry—one of the parent species of the morello and amorella cherries, cultivated for centuries in Europe and Asia. Its many forms include the vigorous marasca, which produces the fruit used in making maraschino liqueur. In the case of Semperflorens, fruiting is limited to a few sour black or dark red cherries which sometimes appear during the summer, while the tree is still in flower. It has been planted quite widely in the USA during the past two centuries, where it is popular, with its neat silhouette, as a leafy shade tree. If, on occasion, it should produce suckers around its base, these must be removed.

The red buckeye, *Aesculus pavia*, a native of the southern USA, is hardy at least in the south and west of Britain. It displays its beautiful crimson candle flowers in June. The leaves, though very distinctive, are not as large as most others of the horse chestnut or buckeye genus, and the shade they cast during the summer is not heavy enough to preclude underplanting with shrubs.

Pyrus salicifolia Pendula, the weeping willow-leaved pear with its

91

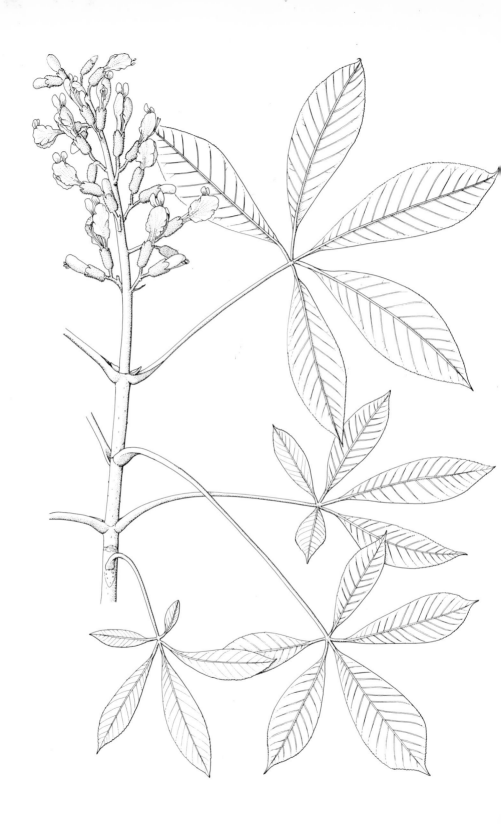

beautiful silvery foliage that rustles in every breeze, has become very popular in England as an alternative to the full-sized weeping willow for planting in small gardens. Its graceful foliage and pendulous habit are perfect to counterbalance the rather rigid cherry leaves, and the clusters of white pear blossom make a fine display in April. A native of the hilly regions of the Black Sea, this little tree is tolerant of extremes, both in climate and soil. There are no true pears native to North America, but they take readily to cultivation there, and *P. s.* Pendula grows well in the eastern United States and in Canada.

A very striking combination of leaf shape and colour can be made by planting the European variegated ivy *Hedera helix* Gold Heart, and allowing it to run where it will below these trees and climb up their stems. It can always be cut back if it climbs too vigorously, but it is unlikely to swamp any in this group, for the small-leaved variegated ivies do not climb as vigorously as the wild green kinds. The name Gold Heart describes the leaves, with their large gold blotch surrounded by dark green margins, and this is one of the handsomest of foliage plants, giving a charming overall effect beneath the dark greens of the summer foliage, the silver of the weeping pear, and the red autumn tints of the maple. Gold Heart is equally vivid throughout the winter months, so that a group thus adorned will present a memorable sight all the year round.

A bold display of colour

From left to right: *Rhus typhina*
  Cotinus coggygria Royal Purple
  Cercis siliquastrum
  Robinia pseudoacacia Frisia
  Tamarix pentandra

This group will grow in full sun in any ordinary garden soil.

The tallest member of the group is the Judas tree, *Cercis siliquastrum*, one of the most spectacular of garden trees in May, when the branches become covered, just as the leaves are opening, with masses of pea-family flowers of a bright pinkish purple. Later in the year, these develop into flat 10cm (4in) purplish pods which festoon the tree. It is handsome in summer foliage too, with large, heart-shaped leaves of a mellow sage green. A native of southern Europe and Asia, the Judas tree is perfectly hardy in Britain and much of the USA. It was introduced into England during the sixteenth century, when

(Opposite) Aesculus pavia

Cercis siliquastrum

legend had it that this was the tree from which Judas Iscariot hanged himself.

Robinia pseudoacacia, the false acacia from the eastern USA, has many varieties, but none are more colourful than Frisia, one of the yellowest of all trees in foliage, with a bright hue that lasts unaltered from spring until autumn. It does not grow so large as a typical false acacia, and is often planted as a solitary specimen tree—perhaps in the centre of a lawn—where its colour and graceful beauty can be admired without competition or distraction. In this group, the brilliance of its yellow foliage is intensified by the contrasting colours of the neighbouring trees.

The purple-leaved smoke tree, *Cotinus coggygria* Royal Purple, has leaves of bright claret purple, brightening slightly to a rich crimson as the summer closes. It is called the smoke tree because of the clouds of hazy purple-grey flower clusters that are on show from the end of the summer until leaf fall in the autumn. This is a picturesque little tree in branch and bark, too, but it needs encouraging, when newly planted, to produce the single strong stem that will form the bole of a standard

94

(Left) The bright yellow foliage of *Robinia pseudoacacia* Frisia, a variety of the false acacia, is intensified by a dark background

(Right) Cotinus coggygria, the smoke tree, needs training if it is to produce a standard stem. The variety Royal Purple is one of the most colourful of small trees

tree. With a little persuasion in the opposite direction, it will creep along the ground as a prostrate shrub—an effect described in one of the groups under Plan 9.

This selection is bounded on the one hand by *Rhus typhina*, the stag's horn sumach, with its strangely thick, hairy twigs, tipped with their prominent, cylindrical flower clusters, and its large leaves which take on brilliant scarlet and crimson autumn colours; on the other hand, there is the delicately foliaged tamarisk, *Tamarix pentandra*, covered during the late summer and autumn with bright pink feathery flower clusters.

Such overall brightness of tree colour needs no additional flowers at ground level. The best possible foil for this group would be a dark evergreen frame of foliage: at ground level, perhaps, the creeping yew *Taxus baccata* Repandens, or the dark-leaved Portugal laurel, *Prunus lusitanica*, trained to grow as a ground-covering shrub.

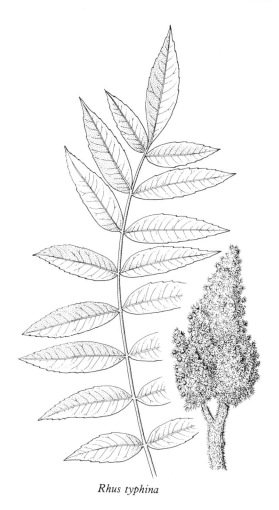

Rhus typhina

Plan 8
Groups of three, spreading to a total width of 12m (40ft)

An arrangement of three rather spreading but firmly textured trees, to form a solid clump or screen. Their spread can be limited by systematically removing the lowest branches as the trees mature. Actual space required on the ground is 7m (23ft) by 3.75m (12ft).

A collection of crabapples

From left to right: *Malus florentina*

                       Malus prunifolia Fastigiata

                       Malus spectabilis

Plan 8—Groups of three trees, spreading to a total width of 12m (40ft)

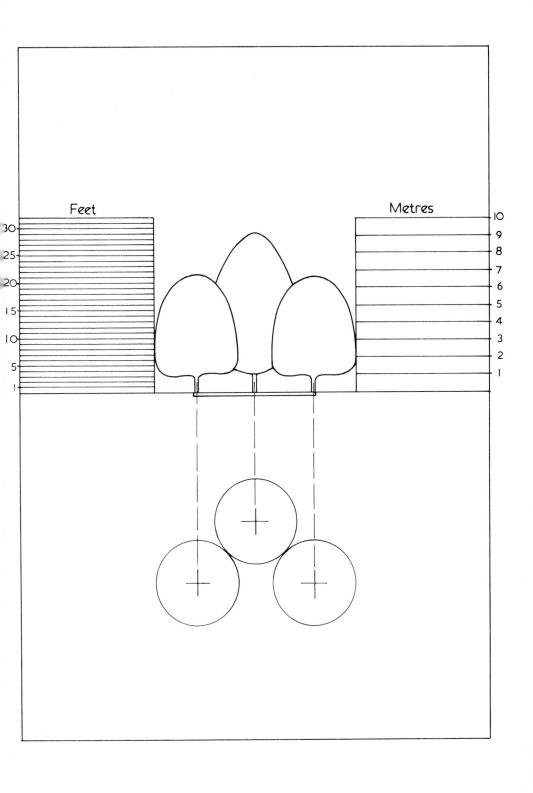

Feet

Metres

30
25
20
15
10
5
1

10
9
8
7
6
5
4
3
2
1

This group of crabs needs a sunny site to grow well and to enable the trees to retain their neat, symmetrical shapes. Any ordinary garden soil is suitable.

First to flower is *Malus prunifolia,* which has been admired in April since its introduction from north-eastern Asia two hundred years ago. The upright variety Fastigiata has the gorgeous pink blossom typical of the species, followed later in the year by red, berry-like fruits. As the tree ages, the branches will tend to spread until the crown is nearly 7m (23ft) wide, unless it is pruned judiciously after flowering has finished in the early summer, selecting the longest branches for removal. It is better to remove whole branches rather than simply to shorten them, not because the tree will suffer damage as a consequence, but because it will tend to develop a proliferation of twiggy shoots at the severed branch tips, and these will be an unsightly nuisance.

M. spectabilis is a long-cultivated Chinese tree, noted for its display of large, pale pink flowers in late April and early May, and these are followed later in the summer and autumn by small yellow apples. One of the best known and most popular of the crabs in Britain, *M. spectabilis* is perfectly hardy, and tolerant of a wide range of soils when grown as an isolated specimen tree.

M. florentina is a southern European crab whose hawthorn-like foliage colours strongly before falling in the autumn, and the typical white apple blossom in May is succeeded by tiny red fruits. This also is a tough little tree which will thrive in poor soils and on exposed sites, though it grows taller in the south of England than it does in the north, and it can be relied on to develop its distinctive, symmetrically domed silhouette.

Trees of this type lend themselves well to adoption by one of the climbing hydrangeas: *Hydrangea petiolaris,* with huge, greenish white flowers in June; *H. anomala,* with similar but smaller flowers, also in June; or the evergreen *H. integerrima,* whose clusters of creamy white flowers appear in August. Crabapples need the sun in order to delight passers-by with their display of white and pastel pink in the spring, but these hydrangeas prefer a modicum of shade. They can be planted nearby and trained up the tree stems until they are firmly established beneath the sheltering canopy—an interesting way to extend the flowering season.

(Opposite) The Chinese foxglove tree, *Paulownia tomentosa,* is perfectly hardy, but needs a sheltered garden in order to flower well

Three rare berrying trees

From left to right: *Sorbus bristoliensis*

$\qquad\qquad\qquad\qquad$ *Malus sikkimensis*

$\qquad\qquad\qquad\qquad$ *Sorbus insignis*

These unusual flowering and berrying trees need a sheltered garden in a reasonably mild climate, though they are happy to grow in either acid or alkaline soils. A sunny, sloping site is best, so that dangerously cold, frosty air can drain freely away in the spring.

Sorbus bristoliensis is a British whitebeam that occurs naturally only in a tiny area—the Avon gorge near Bristol city—and it is very closely related to the common whitebeam, *S. aria*. It has rounded leaves, olive green on their upper surfaces, downy and grey underneath, compactly arranged in a neat, domed crown. A beautiful tree in late May, when the flat clusters of white flowers nestle among the foliage, it is at its most handsome in the autumn with a display of bright orange berries.

Malus sikkimensis is a crabapple from the mountains of northern India, introduced to Britain early in Queen Victoria's reign. Its handsome, upright stance is distinctive enough for it to be used as a solitary specimen tree on a sunny site, and it is very pretty in the spring when laden with white blossom. Later in the summer it is decked with small red berry-like apples.

Sorbus insignis is a rowan from the mountains of Assam, less hardy than most of its genus, but able to thrive at least in southern England and the south-eastern United States. It is a very handsome tree, worth growing in those areas that will support it, with its close head of purplish branches, dark shiny green leaves with contrasting grey undersides, clusters of white flowers in May, and large bunches of pink berries which usually last well on the bare branches over winter. Although, like others of the mountain ash type, *S. insignis* will tolerate many kinds of soil, it needs a sunny site, well sheltered from the worst of the winter's weather.

Provided these trees have full standard or, at least, half standard length stems, so that their lowest branches are not too near the ground, there are several herbaceous ground covering plants that would associate with them well, particularly those which are able to display a drift of colour during the summer before the ornamental

(Opposite above) Prunus Kanzan is probably the best known of the Japanese flowering cherries and a favourite garden tree

(Opposite below) The spreading branches of *Prunus* Accolade, a hybrid cherry, are made to weep during April by the weight of blossom

berries have developed. Some of the saxifrages might serve the purpose, and the hybrid London pride would be ideal, with its dainty pink flowers suspended over a neat, closely growing mat of rosetted leaves.

Three unusual American trees

From left to right: *Aesculus glabra*
Halesia monticola vestita
Aesculus californica

The two horse chestnuts, or buckeyes, and the snowdrop tree, which together form the triple-domed silhouette of this group, all prefer a reasonably sunny garden with an acid soil.

The flowering season for these three trees in succession lasts from early May until August. First to flower is the mountain snowdrop tree, *Halesia monticola*, a native of the south-eastern USA, which displays clusters of white, or occasionally pink, drooping bell-shaped flowers which cover the branches in early May before the leaves have fully opened. In its native habitat it may attain large tree size but, in other areas, though very hardy and adaptable to a wide range of conditions, it rarely exceeds the dimensions of this plan.

The Ohio buckeye, *Aesculus glabra*, has a wider range in the USA than its vernacular name suggests, and it is native to several states in the central and south-eastern parts of the country. When planted away from home, it is quite hardy in other areas of North America, and in the British Isles, where it was first introduced some two hundred years ago. It is an attractive little tree throughout the year, with creamy flowers in May and June, and slender, pointed, palmate leaves which colour richly in the autumn before falling to reveal the picturesquely rough, fissured bark.

Following the Ohio buckeye in flower, the Californian buckeye, *A. californica* produces fragrant pink flower candles which are a delight to see in July and August, and these are succeeded by little pear-shaped conkers. It also is hardy over a wide range of sites, and has been grown in England for many years. One occasionally sees quite old trees which have retained a shrub-like stature but, in its typical form, Californian buckeye makes a neat little tree, with rounded leaflets to match its rotund crown of branches.

Such a wholly American group needs American plants to associate with it: ground-coverers such as the partridge berry, *Gaultheria procumbens*, a dark evergreen which shows the trees to their best

Aesculus californica

advantage in foliage, flower and winter bark, and also, as a bonus, produces a display of white or pink flowers in July and August, with bright red berries in the autumn.

A striking blend of foliage

From left to right: *Acer glabrum*
                     Sorbus × *thuringiaca*
                     Salix alba Sericea

This is one of the hardiest of selections. All these little trees ask is a moderately open site; they are able to grow in garden conditions in any temperate part of the world.

The rock maple, *Acer glabrum*, is a native of the Rocky Mountains and the Cascade Range in the United States and, in a very closely related form of the species, is found as far north as Alaska. This tough little tree was introduced into Britain a century or more back, and its performance has been somewhat variable because individual specimens sometimes retain a shrubby habit of growth. More typically, however, it develops a small tree shape with a compact,

103

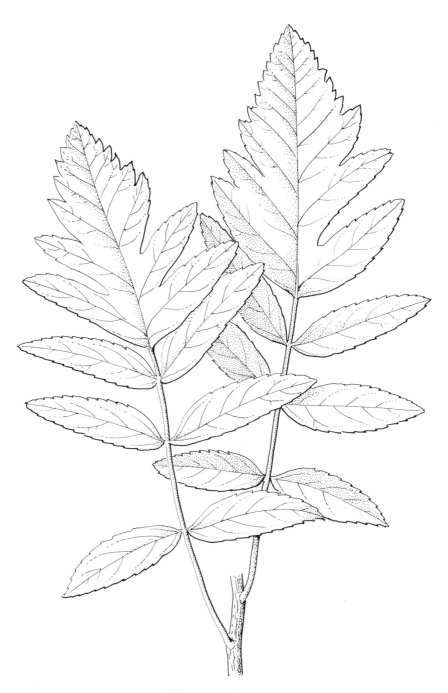

Sorbus × *thuringiaca*

domed crown. Branches arising from ground level and threatening to compete with the main stem should be removed during the late summer. The leaves are usually three-lobed—sometimes completely divided into three leaflets—and occasionally five-lobed, measuring about 13cm (5in) across. The spring flowers are not particularly noticeable, but the rather bandy-legged seed wings have a pinkish tinge which draws the attention of passers-by in the summer.

Sorbus x *thuringiaca* is a hybrid between the European mountain ash, familiar as a wild tree in Britain, especially the north of England, Wales and Scotland, and the whitebeam, often seen growing wild in southern England. On sites where the two parent species occur close together, this little tree sometimes appears naturally, recognisable by the very symmetrical silhouette of its densely branched, compact crown and by the leaves, somewhat intermediate between those of the parents, with a rather olive shade of green on their upper surfaces and grey underneath. The greenish-white flowers in early May, though pleasant, are not very conspicuous. The berries which follow later in the season are more often noticed as they hang on the branches after the leaves have fallen for the winter. They, too, are intermediate between those of their parents, and the bright scarlet is subdued with a few brown speckles. While the rowan by nature inhabits damp, acid soils, the whitebeam prefers drier, sometimes chalky sites, and these preferences are reflected by *S.* x *thuringiaca* in its extreme hardiness and willingness to grow and thrive over a wide range of conditions.

The wild European white willow is not suitable for planting near buildings as it is liable, during spells of dry weather, to draw moisture from the clay beneath the foundations, causing structural damage; but the silver variety, *Salix alba* Sericea, is much smaller, less vigorous, and unlikely to prove a hazard in this direction. It forms a neatly mounded dome, with an even, densely textured foliage of an intense silvery tone. The coloured bark varieties of the species, Chermesina and Vitellina, which are both included in other groups, could be used as an alternative to Sericea. They would provide an interesting cloud of colour during the winter months and, for this purpose, they would not need to be coppiced or pollarded as described for the winter colour arrangements in Plans 3 and 13. However, an unpollarded *S. a.* Sericea, in full leaf during the summer months, is one of the most striking trees to associate with others of contrasting colour and texture.

An area on the sunny side of this group could well be given over to some of the ground-covering heaths and heathers, a combination to stress the tamed wilderness suggested by these trees. Heather blossom, selected, perhaps, to give colour and interest throughout the year, would harmonise beautifully with the dull green, grey and silvery tones predominant in the tree foliage. Most heathers need an acid soil, but *Erica herbacea* (syn. *E. carnea*) the mountain heath, is tolerant of lime. Among the many named varieties of *E. herbacea*, the prostrate, spreading Springwood White and Springwood Pink flower very early in the year, and there are numerous others to follow them in sequence.

A beautiful group at all seasons

From left to right: *Malus floribunda*
                       Acer davidii George Forrest
                       Prunus Accolade

This group is for an open, sunny site, with any reasonable garden soil.

First of the group to flower is *Prunus* Accolade, said to be one of several hybrids between the spring cherry *P. subhirtella*, and the magnificent *P. sargentii*. One of the best ornamental cherries of its size, Accolade has received several garden awards for its bright pink semi-double flowers which are produced in large drooping clusters in April, so profusely that the weeping tendency of the long, flexible branches is exaggerated by the sheer weight of blossom. It is a handsome tree also in the autumn, when the large leaves colour orange and bronze, and in the winter whenever the sun strikes the rich brown bark.

Following in sequence is *Malus floribunda*, a Japanese crabapple which has become an established favourite in England since its introduction early in the reign of Queen Victoria. One of the earliest of the crabs, its flowering season commences usually in the first week of May, the blossom rich crimson in the bud, opening to pale pink or white. Young specimens sometimes tend to develop their crowns at the expense of stem, and so retain a shrubby appearance for several years; to counter this tendency, early development should be guided by removing the lowest branches each year until the clear stem is long enough to support the freely arching silhouette. It is a wonderfully hardy tree, tolerant of a wide range of soils and sites, but blossoming may be curtailed, or prevented altogether, if there is overhead shade. Late summer and autumn sees the branches decorated with red and yellow fruits, no larger than berries.

The maple of the group also produces flowers in May—pendulous clusters of yellowish blossom—but these are unspectacular, though pretty in close-up. George Forrest is a vigorous variety of Father David's maple from the Chinese mountains, and is a very ornamental tree with its large, unlobed, dark green leaves on bright red stalks, and the clusters of red-tinged winged seeds that are on display in the late summer. The bark is conspicuously striped in green and white, and always draws attention during the winter months. It is not lacking the maple tradition of bright autumn foliage colour, for the leaves, though they lack the lobed shape typical of the genus, turn to glorious shades of red and orange before they fall. Fully hardy in Britain and the eastern United States, this is one of the best all-round maples for garden use.

The trees in this group will be flattered if flowering bulbs are naturalised around their stems, especially with the accent on white, yellow and blue. With drifts of snowdrops, chionodoxas, spring and autumn crocuses, dwarf daffodils, bluebells and grape hyacinths, the view will never be dull.

Plan 9
Groups of six, spreading to a total width of 13m (43ft)

A compact screen that will look equally good from front or rear, with an actual planted ground area of 10.5m (35ft) by 3.5m (11ft).

A representative collection of maples

From left to right: *Acer davidii* Madeline Spitta
Acer rubrum Schlesingeri
Acer crataegifolium
Acer davidii Ernest Wilson
Acer micranthum
Acer japonicum Aureum

This is a group which will not object to overall light shade, and some side shade will certainly be beneficial. The group layout is reversible and, if one end of the site is deeper in shade than the other, *Acer japonicum* Aureum should be planted for preference at the shadier end. Any normal garden soil will be suitable.

Father David's maple, *A. davidii*, was represented in the previous plan by its vigorous form George Forrest. In this group, two more distinctive varieties of the species will fit admirably into the arrangement. *A. davidii* itself, from the mountains of central and south-western China, was named in honour of l'Abbé Armand David,

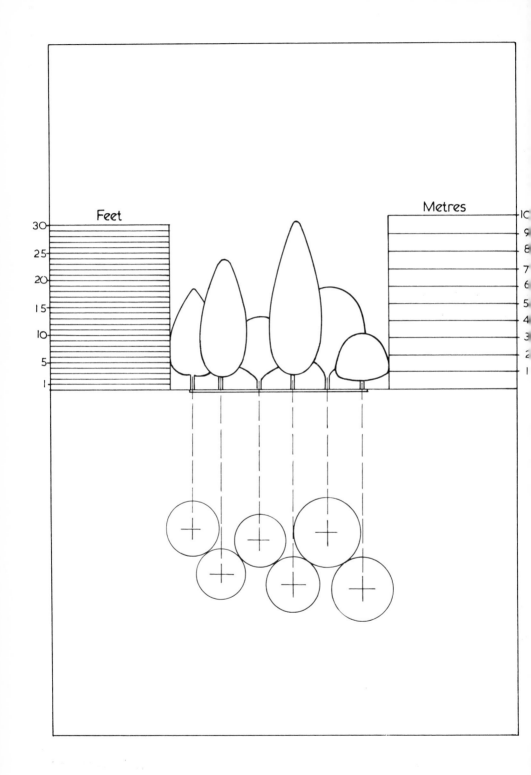

Feet

Metres

Acer japonicum Aureum. This maple needs a fairly well shaded site to retain the soft canary yellow of its foliage

the French missionary and naturalist of the nineteenth century. Its rounded leaves, quite unlike those of most maples, are glossy and dark green during the summer, but with a distinct reddish tinge as they are developing in the spring, and rich scarlet and orange colours in the autumn, when the branches become festooned with pinkish winged seeds. When the leaves fall, the bark is fully revealed, with its remarkable stripes in green and white. The variety Madeline Spitta has a closely columnar form, and promises not to grow too large for small garden use. The other variety in this selection, Ernest Wilson, was introduced as a wild form at the same time as the typical species, during Queen Victoria's reign. It is quite reliably conical as a young tree, with the branches rising at a steep angle from the stem, but these have a tendency to arch at their tips and spread outwards, so that the crown eventually puts on girth as the tree ages. When this happens in a small garden, middle-aged spread can be reduced by removing the lowest crown limbs, for these heavy branches will be the farthest ranging. The effect of removing them, in terms of light and shade, on

Plan 9—Groups of six trees, spreading to a total width of 13m (43ft)

plants growing underneath and in the surrounding area, will be enormous.

The red maple, *A. rubrum*, has a vast natural spread in North America, bounded by Newfoundland, Florida, Dakota and Texas—a range so varied in geography and climate that the species is sure to be hardy and willing to grow in many different types of soil. Schlesingeri is a form that was selected primarily for the extra brilliance of its scarlet and crimson autumn tints, even brighter than the typical tree, which was given its popular name of red maple in recognition of this striking coloration. *A.r.* Schlesingeri, too, produces reddish flowers in the spring, and the winged seed keys later in the year are also a rather dull red.

A. crataegifolium, the hawthorn-leaved maple from Japan, is an attractive tree throughout the year, even when naked for the winter, with its compact outline and handsomely striped bark in white and purplish green. The small and rather variable leaves are reminiscent of a hawthorn, and there are yellow flowers in the spring, arranged along the branches in drooping clusters. A variegated form, Veitchii, is sometimes available from nurseries, and this is a particularly striking little tree, with pink and white markings on the leaves.

Another maple from Japan, and one which has been grown in Western gardens for many years, is *A. micranthum*, with a graceful, almost candelabra-like outline. It has ornamental foliage of small, five-lobed leaves, and clusters of pale flowers in the spring, followed by aeroplane-propeller keys in the autumn. These seed keys, with their widely splayed angle, are similar to those of the final maple of the group: *A. japonicum* Aureum—one of the shapeliest and most tree-like of *A. japonicum* varieties, its beautifully lobed leaves coloured a soft canary yellow throughout the spring and summer. It needs a fairly well shaded site to retain this colour fully, as it tends to scorch along the leaf margins if subjected to strong sunlight. The clusters of purple flowers before the leaves are open add to the spring attractions of the group.

Supporting plants should be planned to continue the woodland theme in foliage texture and colour. The purple-leaved smoke tree, *Cotinus coggygria* Royal Purple, is described under Plan 7 as a beautiful little tree in its own right, but it can very happily be trained as a ground-cover plant, by encouraging the spreading, trailing branches to carpet the ground in front of the maples. The visual harmony is perfectly tuned between this and the yellow-leaved *Acer japonicum* Aureum.

Woodlanders with white flowers and handsome foliage

From left to right: *Eucryphia* × *intermedia* Rostrevor
                               Oxydendrum arboreum
                               Styrax serrulata
                               Amelanchier laevis
                               Staphylea pinnata
                               Cornus kousa

This woodland group needs a slightly acid soil, preferably peaty and moist, and a site that is sheltered from strong winds and lightly shaded, perhaps by tall trees growing nearby.

An amazing sequence of graceful white flowers is on display, from April right through the summer until September, from the trees in this handsome group. First to flower in April is *Amelanchier laevis*, a small tree from eastern North America, perfectly hardy in Britain and grown by British gardeners for more than a century. Clusters of fragrant white anemone-like flowers are on display just as the leaves are opening and last into May, delightfully framed by the purplish tinge of the young spring foliage. The leaves become green during the summer, and take on rich scarlet tints for the autumn. The tree sometimes bears little black berries—'juneberries'—which are edible and very sweet.

Drooping clusters of white flowers lasting from May into June are arranged among the ash-like leaves of *Staphylea pinnata*, a species of bladdernut from central Europe, naturalised in Britain for several centuries. It is a shrubby little tree that forms a symmetrical, rounded fan silhouette and, though it needs a fertile soil and enjoys woodland conditions, it has no objection to the sunshine.

June sees the appearance of the striking, cross-shaped white flower bracts of *Cornus kousa*, one of the dogwoods from the Far East, a useful if somewhat shrubby plant for reasonably good, deep soils, and perfectly hardy in Western gardens. The flowers are followed later in the year by small red fruits, and the species usually adds to the autumn scene by producing vivid crimson and tawny foliage tints.

From June into July, the Himalayan snowbell *Styrax serrulata* presents its display of bell-shaped white flowers which hang in clusters along the leafy shoots. The foliage is handsome too, the dark glossy green, rounded leaves, with their contrasting downy white undersurface, densely arranged in a low, wide-spreading fan. It is a very hardy little tree that will thrive in most parts of Europe and North America, provided it is given a lime-free soil.

The sorrel tree *Oxydendrum arboreum*, from the eastern United

111

Cornus kousa

Oxydendrum arboreum

States, flowers in July and August, with clustered rows of white bells arranged along the shoots. Its vernacular name comes from the bitter but not unpleasant taste of the pointed leaves, which have been used in the kitchen. It was introduced into Britain midway through the eighteenth century and, given the lime-free peaty soil and semi-shaded woodland environment that it likes, the sorrel tree—though not well known by English gardeners—always draws attention in the autumn with its magnificent crimson and gold leaf colours.

Last of the group to flower is *Eucryphia* × *intermedia* Rostrevor, which is covered with its large, yellow-centred white flowers in August and September. It is a hybrid between a South American and a Tasmanian species, an unusual and very beautiful little tree that appreciates woodland conditions and a moist, lime-free soil. It sometimes keeps its leaves in mild winters, but more often than not it is deciduous in Britain and North America. Nevertheless, it is hardy in all except the coldest districts.

Peat added to the soil will help greatly to retain the moisture that these trees need, and it will be quite likely to improve the autumn leaf colours, for some observers claim that this annual display is often brighter on acid rather than alkaline soils.

The predominant colours of this group throughout the season are white and green, turning in the autumn to red and gold. If some kind of blue flower colour can be introduced, this will make an ideal combination. Bluebells, of course, can be used in the spring—the flowers of the bladdernut are reminiscent of white bluebell spikes—but, for long summer flowering, some of the hydrangeas are perfect for building a shrubby foundation. In these acid woodland soils, many hydrangea varieties will take on a blue colour, and there are some lacecaps such as Bluewave and Bluebird which are naturally blue, and will add to the woodland atmosphere by looking completely at home under these circumstances.

Whitebeams and rowans with striking berries

From left to right: *Sorbus* × *thuringiaca* Fastigiata

                 Sorbus commixta

                 Sorbus graeca

                 Sorbus pohuashanensis

                 Sorbus poteriifolia

                 Sorbus mougeotii

Trees of this genus are renowned for their ability to grow under extreme conditions of poor soil, and climatic or industrial exposure. Given an open, sunny site, they will thrive in any garden.

This beautiful collection will display a subtle range of leafy greens during the summer. As the shady foreground to a low building, this group would be ideally placed. Trees of this genus all flower in the spring and early summer, and the latter half of May sees the whole group white with broad clusters of flowers, individually small, but attractive at close quarters and quietly impressive from a distance. In the autumn, the range of berries through shades of pink, red and orange is quite spectacular as the leaves turn russet and amber, and fall. Specialisation for economic reasons means that not all these trees are readily obtainable from nurseries, and only the largest growers will be able to supply them all.

Sorbus × *thuringiaca*, the natural hybrid between whitebeam and rowan which was included in its typical form under Plan 8, has given

(Opposite) An upright variety of a natural hybrid between whitebeam and rowan, *Sorbus* × *thuringiaca* Fastigiata is one of the best trees to flank a road or driveway

rise to the strictly upright variety Fastigiata. Its narrow, evenly compact crown structure qualifies it as one of the best isolated specimen trees for planting in very restricted spaces—perhaps for flanking a driveway. The leaf colour is a dull green with grey down on the undersides, and autumn sees the display of handsome bunches of speckled red berries. It is quite as hardy as the typical hybrid *S.* × *thuringiaca* and, taking after its two parent species, is able to grow on all types of soil.

S. commixta is a hardy Japanese rowan with quite sweetly scented flowers. It bears the typical mountain ash leaves, a glossy light green in the summer, though with a pronounced coppery hue in the spring, and colouring well with crimson, orange and purple tints in the autumn. As the leaves fall, the tree remains laden with bunches of small orange berries. It, also, is a compact, strictly upright tree, especially in its youth. As it ages, the crown is liable to put on weight and broaden and, if this happens, the lowest branches can be removed.

S. graeca is a whitebeam from Greece and south-eastern Europe, a tree of pleasantly compact appearance in the summer, tolerant of poor soils, and able to grow well in southern England and comparable climatic zones. Its rounded, toothed leaves have a conspicuously downy white undersurface, and it is handsome in the autumn with dark crimson berries. On young trees, the densely twigged crown is narrowly erect, but maturity sees the spread broaden and, with this species too, the lowest limbs are often best removed from mature trees, to raise the crown and reduce the area that is overshadowed.

S. pohuashanensis is a Chinese rowan, one of the hardiest of the mountain ashes, introduced to the West a century ago and thriving in cool and even cold regions, wherever the soil is reasonably moist. The little double-toothed leaves are bright green above and downy grey on their undersides. It is a prolific fruiter, even in exposed or industrially polluted planting sites, and bears spectacularly huge clusters of bright orange berries.

S. poteriifolia is another hardy little rowan from China, rather slow growing, forming a reliably shaped crown of purplish branches, handsome in dark green leaf and when bearing its large clusters of conspicuous pink berries. An easily grown tree, it thrives in any soil, and has often given good results when planted as an isolated specimen in poor, dry places.

S. mougeotii is an Alpine whitebeam from the European mountains, a very hardy little tree that will withstand severe exposure or industrial pollution, and is able to grow on poor, chalky soils. Its broadly lobed

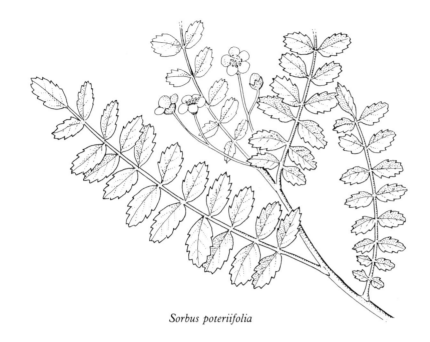

Sorbus poteriifolia

leaves bear the typical whitebeam down on their undersides, and bright red berries are on display during the late summer and autumn.

This is a group for a sunny site, and low carpeting shrubs of the sun-loving kind are ideal to associate with it. Some of the shrubby veronicas have the finely textured, soft grey foliage that will stress the subtle hues of the *Sorbus* leaves and accentuate the bright berry colours. Ground-hugging bushes such as the veronicas *Hebe* × *franciscana* 'Blue Gem', *H.* Bowles Hybrid, *H.* Edinensis and *H. pinguifolia* Pagei are very suitable for the purpose and, being ever-green, will lend interest during the winter months.

Plan 10
Groups of five, spreading to a total width of 14m (46ft)

A grove of trees, rather than a screen, this arrangement will look equally striking from the front or from the rear. The area required on the ground measures 10.75m (35ft) by 6.25m (21ft).

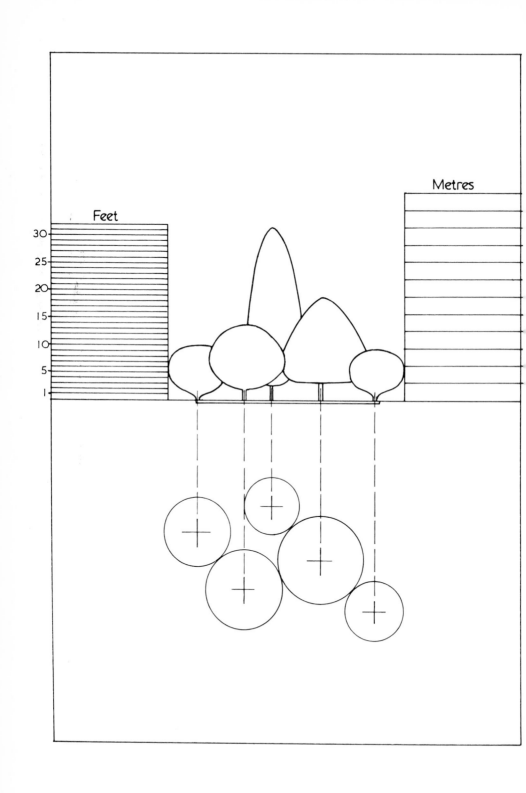

Feet

Metres

30
25
20
15
10
5
1

Collection of magnolias I

From left to right: *Magnolia stellata*

                         Magnolia Charles Coates

                         Magnolia sargentiana

                         Magnolia Kewensis

                         Magnolia stellata Rosea

Magnolias thrive in a woodland environment, with side shade and protection against the worst gales, and the spring-flowering kinds at least fare better in districts which are relatively free from spring frosts. However, they have no objection to town life or industrial pollution, and a sheltered garden in the town will often provide their ideal home. An acid soil is best, fertile and moist, with plenty of peat and other humus addition, but magnolias will tolerate quite heavy clay. Both light and heavy soils on magnolia sites will benefit from dressings of stable manure and similar rich, organic material.

The season of glory for these magnolias is springtime, from March to June. First to flower in March are the two shrubs in the collection: *Magnolia stellata* and its variety *M. stellata* Rosea, to provide an anchor at each end of the group. *M. stellata* is one of the smaller magnolias from Japan, and forms a neat, if rather spreading, mound with a reliably bowl-shaped silhouette which makes it very useful in small gardens. It is hardy and tolerant of a wide range of soil and site conditions, but the fragrant, pure white, multi-petalled flowers are so early, and appear in such profusion, that they really deserve a moderately frost-free site. A sloping garden will often allow petal-shrivelling frosts to roll like cold water down the hill, and it is as well to ensure that no unnecessary obstruction intervenes to check the downward movement of cold air and allow frost layers to build up. Damage is less severe when plants are screened from early morning sunshine, as too quick a thawing process can rupture plant cells and cause blackening of petals and buds. Fortunately, spring frosts do not last long, and so many flowers are produced in succession that most of them manage to escape damage.

The pink-flowered form, *M.s.* Rosea, also becomes covered with sweetly fragrant many-petalled flowers, but of the palest blush, darker on the undersurface of each petal, so that the buds are rose-pink before opening to a full-blown 7 or 8cm (3in). Flowering is finished before the dark green leaves start to open. Rosea tends towards a multi-stemmed, shrubby habit but, like the typical *M. stellata*, it makes a reliably compact shape, though it grows only slowly. Both forms have

Plan 10—Groups of five trees, spreading to a total width of 14m (46ft)

Magnolia stellata

a head start over many magnolias in that their flowers appear while the plants are still quite young.

Flowering in April, the neatly conical little hybrid magnolia Kewensis also produces flowers on young plants—large, pure white and sweetly scented blooms, appearing on the bare branches just before the leaves open. *M.* Kewensis was raised in Kew Gardens as the result of a cross between two Japanese species, and it is perfectly hardy in southern England at least, and capable of thriving on limy soil.

At the end of April and in early May, the leaves have barely started to open when *M. sargentiana* displays its enormous pink flowers. They

(Opposite) Magnolia Charles Coates. A close view of the distinctive late spring flowers of this bushy little hybrid magnolia

do not appear until the tree is several years old, but they are surely worth waiting for, because *M. sargentiana*, of Chinese origin, is a beautiful tree, its conical shape somewhat variable in early years, but always tall and picturesque. It is one of those magnolias—the majority—that need a fertile, acid soil, and will not grow in limy or chalky types.

Carrying the flowering season from the opening green buds of May well into leafy June, *M.* Charles Coates was the result of a union between an American and a Japanese species. It makes a bushy little tree which, though it may retain a shrubby habit, always forms a neatly rounded crown of branches. It will succeed on heavy clay but, like *M. sargentiana*, it will not tolerate lime in the soil.

Magnolia foliage during the flowerless summer months has an interesting range of colour and texture, shades and shapes, from the rounded grey leaves of *M. sargentiana* to the narrow, dark glossy green of *M. stellata* and *M. s.* Rosea.

The early spring flowers of these glorious trees are highlighted and given extra weight if they can be seen over a carpet of blue: the early-flowering *Muscari* grape hyacinths and the sky blue *Chionodoxa luciliae* will provide this colourful foil, if they are massed so as to form a drift beneath the branches.

Collection of magnolias II

From left to right: *Magnolia* × *loebneri*
                    Magnolia salicifolia
                    Magnolia sargentiana robusta
                    Magnolia denudata
                    Magnolia stellata Rubra

Their requirements are the same as those of the previous group. Magnolias such as these can also be grown very successfully against a high wall, but this should not expose them to early morning sunshine. A west-facing aspect often offers the right kind of conditions, but nothing can better an open garden, sited among surrounding woodland trees.

This collection of magnolias flowers mainly during March and April, and includes some of the hardiest and most fragrant of the genus. One of them—*Magnolia* × *loebneri*—will even grow satis-factorily on shallow soils overlying chalk, and this hybrid is also note-worthy for producing its narrow-petalled white flowers on quite young plants. They are very sweetly scented and appear in great profusion in

April, before the leaves open. *M.* × *loebneri* originated as a hybrid between two Japanese species, and makes a bushy little tree with a fairly symmetrical crown shape.

Particularly beautiful in foliage is the willow-leaved *M. salicifolia* from Japan, one of the hardiest of the genus, much planted in Britain and the United States for the best part of a century. It has received several garden awards for its decorative properties; the fragrant white flowers appear in April even on quite young specimens (old trees are absolutely smothered in blossom), and the whole plant gives off a strong scent of lemon if it is bruised. This is one of the magnolias that prefers a moist, peaty soil, and will refuse to grow if any lime is present. Young plants have a somewhat narrow, conical silhouette, but this broadens in maturity to the rounded shape allowed for in this plan. Jermyns, a cultivated variety of *M. salicifolia*, assumes this broader shape at an earlier age, and this tree also has the most beautiful, freely produced flowers, but it is slower growing.

M. sargentiana robusta is a wild subspecies of *M. sargentiana*, which was included in the previous group. It flowers at an earlier age than the type, although the tree nevertheless needs to be several years old before the flowering stage is reached. When this time comes, it produces huge, nodding crimson or deep pink flowers, up to 30cm (12in) across, which open in March and April before the leathery leaves appear. In its native China it makes a sizeable tree, and is inclined to spread broadly from the base. In Britain and the USA, though vigorous, it is more compact, and is hardy in all but the coldest districts.

M. denudata is the yulan, a native of China, where it also makes a fairly large tree, but when planted in Western gardens it usually attains much smaller dimensions, though it spreads in old age. It will not tolerate lime in the soil, but otherwise is one of the hardiest and most easily grown of the Asian magnolias. The fragrant flowers which appear in March and April before the leaves open, are white. The variety of *M. denudata* known as Purple Eye has coloured flowers, but it usually retains shrub-like proportions.

M. stellata Rubra is one of the best low-growing shrubby magnolias from Japan, the branches fanned into a bowl shape which becomes covered, in March and April, with deep pink fragrant flowers, similar to, but more crimson in shade than, those of *M. s.* Rosea. Although a slow growing plant, it is one of the hardiest magnolias, and able to succeed in all types of soil.

If magnolias outspread their site, they can be pruned like fruit trees, cutting the longer branches back to an outward-pointing growth bud or a flower bud spur, as soon as flowering has finished in the early summer. Magnolias which fail to make headway after planting can also be stimulated into growth by heavy pruning. It is normal for new plants to suffer a growth check the first season after planting, but if they still remain comparatively inactive during the second year they should be cut hard back to near ground level early the following spring. The resultant shoots will have to be singled when they have reached a length of about 45cm (18in), if a single stemmed tree is needed, and this will direct the plant's energy into making a strong, standard stem.

The contrast in foliage texture is even more marked with this group than in the previous collection of magnolias, and ranges from the almost oval leaves of *M. denudata* to the slender, willow-like leaves of *M. salicifolia*. During the summer months, the shapely leaves of the hostas, also known as plantain lilies, can be used as a foil for the glossy magnolia foliage, for they grow well in the sort of conditions these trees enjoy. They have the added advantage of producing lily-like purple or white flowers from July to September, and full use can be made of their remarkable variety of leaf size and colour, ranging from the small, narrow, dark green *Hosta lancifolia* and the many variegated forms of intermediate size, such as *H. albomarginata* and *H. crispula*, to the huge, broad, blue grey leaves of *H. glauca* Robusta.

Hardy ornamentals for a tough site

From left to right: *Crataegus intricata*
Crataegus rivularis
Sorbus meinichii
Crataegus chlorosarca
Sorbaronia × *sorbifolia*

This is a collection of particularly hardy little trees, ideal for a dry, exposed site, growing best in full sun, and well able to withstand pollution from industry or exhaust fumes from a busy highway. They are all attractive in leaf, in spring flower, and in late summer or autumn berry.

Crataegus intricata is much smaller than most other hawthorns, a North American native widely distributed in the wild over much of Canada and the eastern USA. It was introduced into Europe early in the eighteenth century, but is only rarely planted in Britain. The white May blossom is followed by tawny red berries in the autumn.

Sorbus meinichii

C. rivularis is unusual among the hawthorns in having its origins in the dry west of the USA, for most of the American members of the genus come from the east. One of the best small trees for withstanding dry soil conditions, it is both utilitarian and beautiful, with white blossom early in June, followed by very dark red—almost black—berries, and handsome, deeply lobed leaves which usually colour brightly before falling in the autumn. Like the previous thorn, it has been planted only rarely in Britain, despite its usefully compact shape, for its upright stance allows it to occupy a small space without crowding.

The third hawthorn of the group is *C. chlorosarca* from the Far East, a useful little tree both for its shapely and upright symmetry, and for its complete indifference to industrial pollution and poor soil conditions. It is usually without thorns and, with its purplish brown twigs, yew-green leaves and deep purple berries, has a strikingly dark appearance throughout the year—a swarthy complexion only heightened by the contrast of white blossom at the end of May.

Another very hardy little tree for cold, exposed or smoky situations is *Sorbus meinichii*, a Norwegian mountain ash, very similar in blossom, in light green leaf and crimson fruit to the British rowan, to which it is very closely related, but the branches and twigs of its crown are more compact and fastigiate.

Sorbaronia × *sorbifolia* is an interesting hybrid between the black chokeberry—a shrub from the eastern USA—and the American mountain ash. It makes a shrubby little tree which combines some of the characteristics of both its parents—a somewhat slow-growing plant, very hardy and able to survive in any soil type. Quite attractive throughout the year, it bears white flowers in the spring followed by black berries, and puts on a good display of scarlet and orange foliage colours in the autumn. The unusual 'wine glass' shape of its fanned crown lends itself to thoughtful planting in small gardens where, as a solitary tree, it can be used to give height to a flower bed without overshading the plants too drastically.

Some of the heavily trailing shrub roses could well be used to front a group like this, for the thorny, sprawling mat of foliage will stress the tough, pioneering aspect of these hardy little trees. The overall effect, through the seasons, of beautiful flowers, fine foliage, and hips, haws and rowan berries fruiting together, will be worthy of the best-kept garden. *Rosa filipes* Kiftsgate is an example of a vigorously sprawling rose, with bright green summer foliage—coppery early in the year—and masses of fragrant white flowers in June and July, followed by countless little dark red hips.

Plan 11
Groups of five, spreading to a total width of 15m (50ft)

An arrangement that will look beautiful from all angles—in a large garden it could form an island bed in a lawn; it could enclose a permanent garden feature; or it could accommodate shrub and herbaceous beds beneath its canopy and between the stems. Actual ground area required measures 11.75m (39ft) by 9.75m (32ft).

Colour and beauty throughout the year

From left to right: *Frangula alnus*
Prunus Shimidsu Sakura
Styrax obassia
Salix × *chrysocoma*
Crataegus laevigata Paul's Scarlet

Plan 11—Groups of five trees, spreading to a total width of 15m (50ft)

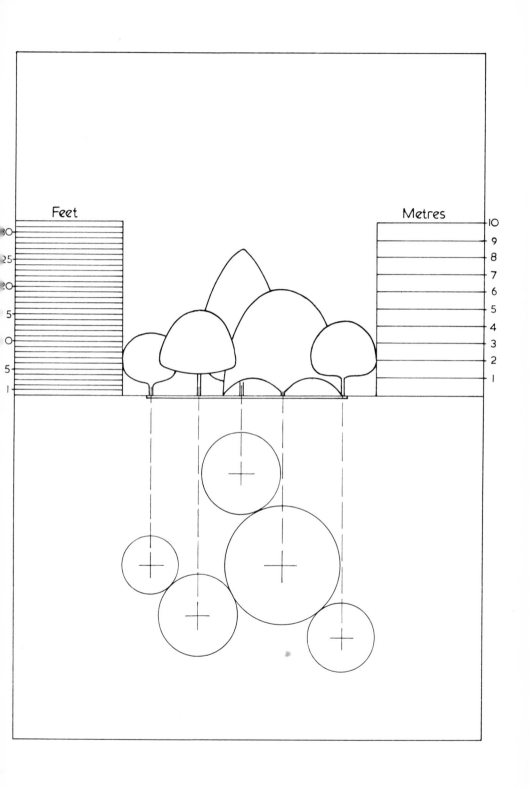

Feet

Metres

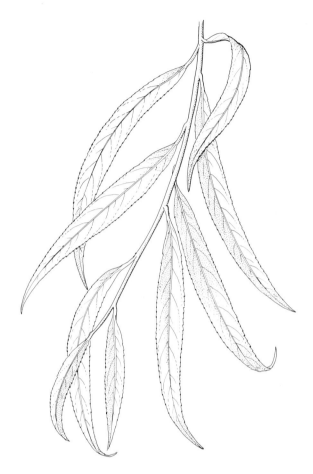

Salix × *chrysocoma*

These trees will grow best on a moist, peaty site, and look most charming in a woodland setting, especially near water, but most soils and sites will support them. They have no objection to light shade, but will also thrive in full sunshine.

The most striking member of this group is the golden weeping willow, *Salix* × *chrysocoma*, potentially somewhat large for the average garden, but too well loved to be omitted from these pages. When it is grown in an arrangement such as this, or when space is restricted, the highest arching branches can be removed every year once the overall height has attained about 4.5m (15ft). This work can be done in the summer, around July. If left until the autumn or winter, it will usually result in a thicket of coppice growth arising near the scar.

Angular height is brought to the group by the Japanese snowbell, *Styrax obassia*, a hardy woodland tree which has been grown in the West for the past century, able to thrive in the sort of site that the American snowbells enjoy, and appreciating a moist, peaty soil. This tree is better if no lime is present, but it will usually stay healthy provided the peat and moisture are there in good measure. The display of snowbells appears in June—fragrant, bell-like white flowers, clustered beneath the large, downy leaves.

These two trees are balanced in outline by the next largest of the group, for the Japanese flowering cherry *Prunus* Shimidsu Sakura has a distinctively flattened crown formation, made almost weeping during late April and early May by the burden of double white flowers in drooping clusters. The buds are pink before they open fully, so there is something of a colour change to add interest to the fresh spring scene, with the copper and sage green of young foliage and the bright yellow of the weeping willow shoots. Shimidsu Sakura is a very hardy little tree which seldom complains about its planting site.

A strong contrast in foliage and habit is supplied by the stiffly rotund shape of *Crataegus laevigata* Paul's Scarlet; from mid May until well into June its mass of double scarlet blossom is seen to perfection, framed against the draped silver and gold of the willow. In the wild, *C. laevigata* is the smaller of the two native British hawthorns, and the parent of most of the cultivated varieties grown in British gardens. As seen in the countryside, it is a charming little tree with masses of white or pale pink blossom, opening in the second half of May. 'May blossom', to recall the old English name for the hawthorn, is supposed traditionally to open on May day, and so it used to do—until the year 1752, when the new Gregorian calendar of 1582 was finally put into effect in England, and caused the date to leapfrog overnight by almost two weeks. *C. laevigata* has long thorns, but it is not as fiercely armed as the larger and commoner of the two British hawthorns, *C. monogyna*. Both are alike in flower and in the outward appearance of their red berries, which provide such a show in the autumn—and a feast for the birds. But, though similar, the two hawthorns may be distinguished by a closer examination of their berries: haws from *C. monogyna* contain only one seed, while those from *C. laevigata* include two, embedded in the pulp. Paul's Scarlet, with its double scarlet flowers, and the variety known as Coccinea Plena are probably identical, and nurseries may sell this little tree under either name.

At the opposite end of the arrangement, a neat little tree with bright

129

Crataegus laevigata Paul's Scarlet is a fully double scarlet variety of the wild British may tree

green, glossy, rounded leaves adds the finishing touch, and lends a sober, well established air to the group. This is *Frangula alnus*, the alder buckthorn, a small European tree native also to Britain. Its flowers are inconspicuous, but the red and black berries are noticeable in the late summer, and autumn sees the handsome foliage turn a clear yellow. In nature, the alder buckthorn shows a predilection for year-round moisture, and is often found growing near the waterside and in damp places, but it is perfectly tolerant of all types of soil, including fairly dry ones.

The choice of trees in this group suggests a gentle, wooded valley with a stream meandering through. The margin of a lake would be an ideal type of environment which would please them all. In a natural setting, such a site might be carpeted with wild garlic, with its drifts of starry white flowers in the spring. Other very suitable ground covering plants would be lilies of the valley, hostas, irises, peonies and ferns.

Spring blossom and contrasting foliage

From left to right: *Prunus × amygdalo-persica* Pollardii
Crataegus × lavallei
Chamaecyparis lawsoniana Pembury Blue
Betula pendula Youngii
Prunus simonii

This collection of very hardy, beautiful trees will thrive in any normal garden soil on an open, sunny site. Overshading will ruin their symmetry, but on the other hand a dark background of trees or tall evergreen shrubs such as laurel or rhododendron will enhance the visual effect. The cypress Pembury Blue should be clothed with foliage to ground level when young, but older specimens are often best pruned to waist height.

Betula pendula is the silver birch—the lady of the woods in Europe and Britain—and its strongly weeping variety Youngii is a valuable garden tree, less well known than the typical birch. The wild species, with its delicate proportions, seems an obvious choice for planting on restricted sites, but in fact it will soon outgrow a small garden. Strongly weeping forms of the tree appear quite frequently in the wild, where their appearance varies considerably from one individual to another. Those labelled Youngii should produce identical results, although their initial height will depend on the length of stem that has been trained upright or used as a grafting standard. In maturity, the tree slowly builds up height as it mounds itself into a dome. The birches are well known for their ability to thrive in poor soils and on exposed sites, but they must not be planted in the shade, and *B. p.* Youngii will lose its shape if expected to grow under overshadowed conditions.

The silver stems of the birch, its light green foliage in the summer, and its weeping veil of reddish twigs in the winter, are backed tellingly in this group by the tall blue spire of the conifer, *Chamaecyparis lawsoniana* Pembury Blue. This is probably the finest silver-blue variety of Lawson's cypress, and with its intense colour and dense foliage makes a perfect foil for the other trees, to stress each nuance of shape and colour. Pembury Blue may be expected eventually to grow quite tall, but it will not outgrow the symmetry of this group, for it

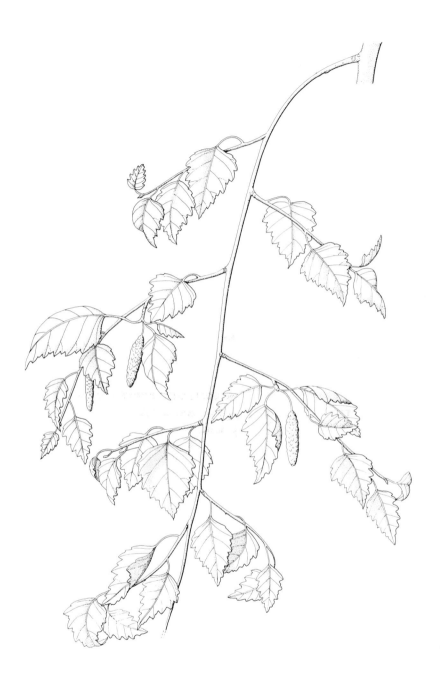

Betula pendula Youngii

(Opposite) Embothrium coccineum lanceolatum, the Norquinco Valley firebush, is one of the showiest of small woodland trees in May and June

retains its proportions well and will never spread too wide across the base.

The third bulkiest tree in this selection is a hawthorn, *Crataegus × lavallei*—a hybrid between the American cockspur thorn and a Mexican species—a tough little tree, well adapted to a wide range of sites and soils, including poor, dry ones. It has few thorns, and a softer texture than most of the genus, with its fairly large, glossy, dark green leaves. The end of May sees it sheeted with white blossom and, late in the year, heavily laden with bright orange berries which persist on the bare branches well into winter.

With an early flowering *Prunus* at either extremity, the group wakes into spring early in March with the fragrant pink flowers, each 5cm (2in) across, of *P. × amygdalo-persica* Pollardii, perhaps the most ornamental of the many hybrids between peach and almond that have been grown in gardens over the centuries. Even grimy industrial sites and cold, exposed places will not inhibit the glorious flowering display of this fine little tree. A dark background will help to bring out the fresh pink of the petals more clearly.

Later in March, and carrying the spring flowering season into April, the apricot plum *P. simonii* opens its massed white blossom. This tree has a natural range in northern China, and grows well in cold and fairly dry areas—it has been planted quite widely in the western USA for the sake of its fruits, which resemble fragrant Victoria plums. For fruit production, it is often grown in the shape of a broadly conical bush, quite distinct from the standard tree habit intended for this arrangement.

Such a well proportioned group as this, ideal for all-round viewing, might make an island bed set in a lawn, and flower beds are often used to fill in temporarily until the trees are several years old. Predominantly orange and yellow flowers will be perfect: orange wallflowers, marigolds, flame-coloured dahlias, yellow and orange chrysanthemums. These are colours which blend with the blue cypress and never clash, despite their brilliance, with the silvery white of the birch stems, which some colours can tend to vulgarise.

Spring flowers and blending foliage

From left to right: *Prunus cerasifera* Pendula
Malus toringoides

(Opposite) Sorbus meinichii is a Norwegian mountain ash which will thrive in cold, exposed or smoky situations

> *Ostrya japonica*
> *Davidia involucrata*
> *Malus* Echtermeyer

This group needs a moderately fertile, loamy soil, with some shelter from cold winds, but without overhead shade.

In this selection, a large weeping tree has not been used, as in the two previous groups, to bulk the design. Instead, the weeping element is provided at each end of the arrangement with two smaller, spring-flowering trees: a cherry plum and a crabapple.

First of these is the weeping myrobalan, *Prunus cerasifera* Pendula, in outline virtually the same as the upright form Nigra, but with each twig and slender branch drooping at its extremity to give, overall, a very beautiful effect. One of the purple-leaved varieties of *P. cerasifera* could be used instead, and the results would be equally charming, but the green-leaved *P. c.* Pendula—wreathed in white flowers during March and April before the leaves open—is a superbly ornamental little tree. There are several varieties of the species, many of which are rather similar, and they may find themselves mislabelled by some nurseries.

The weeping tree at the far end of the group is *Malus* Echtermeyer, a very graceful little crabapple with wide-spreading, drooping branches and leaves of a lovely bronzy purple. In early May the slender shoots are laden with crimson blossom, followed later in the year by purple berries. Echtermeyer, or a very similar little tree, is sometimes sold under the name of *M. purpurea* Pendula.

Another, rather larger crabapple with a more rigidly spreading, somewhat bushy crown, is the Chinese *M. toringoides*, which was introduced to the West at the turn of the twentieth century and has become quite popular in America and Britain. It has received garden awards for its ornamental qualities—its elegant habit, the beauty of its clustered creamy white blossom in mid May, the striking red and yellow berries which follow and, as a bonus, the bright autumn colours which illuminate its lobed leaves. It is a tough little tree, well able to grow on comparatively poor, dry sites, provided it is not overshaded.

An informally rotund crown shape to bulk the design is provided by *Davidia involucrata*, discovered for the West by the missionary and plant collector l'Abbé David, and brought out of China during the nineteenth century, when the genus was named in his honour. It is a hardy tree, revelling in light woodland conditions and thriving in any loamy soil that does not dry out too severely during the summer. In

Davidia involucrata

leaf, it looks not unlike a lime of the genus *Tilia*, but it is unmistakable in the spring when arrayed with the large white involucres, or flower bracts, that have been likened to freshly laundered pocket handkerchiefs hanging from the tree to dry, and which gave the tree its vernacular name—the handkerchief tree.

A pleasantly green cone to give height and depth to the arrangement is found in *Ostrya japonica*, the hop hornbeam which comes from Japan and the east coast of China. It is planted but rarely in Western gardens, though it is often obtainable from nurserymen, and grows easily in most situations and any reasonably fertile soil. It provides a focus of interest in the autumn, when it is covered with its intriguing green hops.

The domed, rounded aspect of this group will be carried down to ground level very successfully if the hybrid shrub *Hypericum* Hidcote is planted generously beneath the canopy. This compactly rounded bush becomes covered with glorious golden yellow flowers which last

137

from high summer to autumn. It grows readily on all kinds of soil, and is ideal beneath deciduous trees to bridge the gap between sun and shade, and between woodland grove and flower border.

Plan 12
Groups of five, spreading to a total width of 16m (53ft)

A planting design incorporating a V-formation, ideal to flank a garden feature or conceal a small building, and intended for viewing from the front. The actual ground plan measures 10.5m (35ft) by 7m (23ft).

Quiet colours with blending foliage textures

From left to right: *Elaeagnus pungens* Maculata
                     Chamaecyparis lawsoniana Columnaris
                     Amelanchier florida
                     Malus Katherine
                     Acer ginnala

This charming group will grow in any reasonable soil, and the best results will be seen in a sunny garden. The cypress Columnaris should not be stem pruned, and the vigorous shrub *Elaeagnus* should also be branched to the ground. The design may be reversed if necessary so that the evergreen flank can provide the optimum shelter from winter winds.

Acer ginnala, a maple from the Far East, made its way to Western gardens midway through the nineteenth century, and has proved itself hardy and tolerant of a wide range of soils and sites in Britain and the eastern USA. A slenderly branched tree of elegant proportions, it wafts a little perfume on the air during May from its otherwise inconspicuous flowers, and is very handsome in foliage, with bright green, three-lobed leaves which become scarlet, crimson and orange in the autumn before they fall.

Autumn colour is also particularly pronounced—a harmonious bright yellow—in the rounded leaves of the juneberry, *Amelanchier florida*, which comes from the western USA rather than Florida, the specific name referring not to the state but to the juneberry's free-flowering habit, for it is delightful in the spring when laden with its white flowers. It grows well in Britain and, unlike others of its genus, will thrive in limy soils. It often tends to adopt a shrubby habit and

(Opposite) Hypericum Hidcote is an ideal shrub to bridge the gap between sun and shade, and between woodland grove and flower border

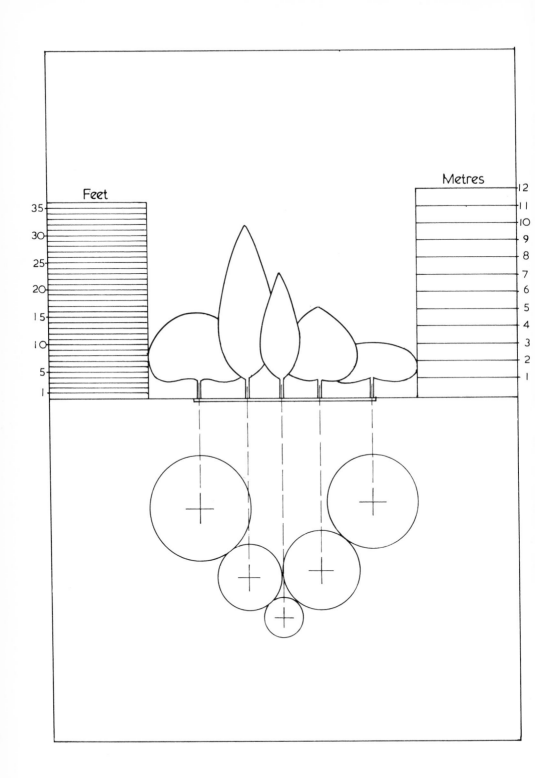

Feet

Metres

35
30
25
20
15
10
5
1

12
11
10
9
8
7
6
5
4
3
2
1

The semi-double blossom of this hybrid crabapple, *Malus* Katherine, opens pink, soon fading to white

can readily be grown as a multi-stemmed tree, but if, by this style of growth, it threatens to outspread its allotted site, some of these stems will have to be removed.

Malus Katherine is a hybrid crabapple which produces a charming display of semi-double blossom, opening pink and fading to white. It is hardy over much of Europe and North America, though it probably descended from Far Eastern crabapple species. It is perfectly happy in poor soil, provided it is not too dry, and the site allows its neatly proportioned crown to feel the sunshine.

Elaeagnus pungens is a large and vigorous evergreen Japanese shrub which was introduced to the West early in the nineteenth century. Its variety Maculata, also known as Aureo-variegata, has glossy leaves

Plan 12—Groups of five trees, spreading to a total width of 16m (53ft)

Elaeagnus pungens Maculata

brightly splashed with gold, a colour which persists throughout the year and glows during the darkest days of winter. It grows well in all but chalk soils, and has no objection to a modicum of shade.

Towering height in this group is added by a Dutch variety of the western North American Lawson's cypress, *Chamaecyparis lawsoniana* Columnaris—a variety which, since its distribution after World War II, has become very popular in Britain and America. One of the most reliably symmetrical pillar shapes among the many Lawson's varieties, it is unlikely ever to outgrow its site. The foliage has a rather olive shade of green, with a greyish bloom on the under-surface of the leaf sprays.

All these neat plants need a sunny site to look their best, and similarly, on their sunny side at least, the small plants to accompany them should be sun-lovers too. *Geranium endressii* varieties will all bloom throughout the summer: A. T. Johnson, with silvery pink flowers; Claridge Druce, with large magenta flowers—this one can be allowed to run freely in the shady patches; Rose Clair, with crimson veined white flowers; and Wargrave Pink, with pure pink flowers.

142

Other choices include the geranium hybrid Russell Prichard, which makes a close, grey-green carpet with long-lasting magenta flowers, and *Geranium wallichianum* Buxton's Blue, violet blue with a white eye, which comes into flower during the late summer and autumn.

A striking blend of colours

From left to right: *Cornus controversa*
Fagus sylvatica Purple Dawyck
Chamaecyparis lawsoniana Fletcheri
Robinia pseudoacacia Bessoniana
Chionanthus virginicus

This is a distinguished collection which will thrive in a sunny garden, with any normal soil. The cypress Fletcheri must be allowed to retain its foliage to ground level.

Cornus controversa is a vigorous Japanese dogwood with distinctive, horizontally tiered branches that become covered in May with clusters of small, cream coloured flowers, followed by black berries in the autumn. The leaves, bright green on their upper surfaces, are grey beneath, and the foliage takes on a crimson-purple autumn coloration to match the adjacent Purple Dawyck beech.

The British beech itself, *Fagus sylvatica*, is a huge forest tree, and the upright-growing green-leaved variety Fastigiata, the Dawyck beech, often planted in gardens, also grows to a considerable size. This purple-leaved form, Purple Dawyck, which was introduced during the 1970s, is unlikely to attain the same stature. There are but few closely columnar trees with purple leaves, and this clone is sure to become very popular for use in small gardens.

Varieties of Lawson's cypress are many and varied, and *Chamaecyparis lawsoniana* Fletcheri is one of the most widely planted as a specimen tree—often on a rock garden, where it soon grows too large for the site. When included in a group such as this, although it may eventually grow taller than the plan intended, it will never spread too wide at the base. Its close, fuzzy grey foliage often conceals multiple stems, but Fletcheri rarely separates, even when weighed down by deep snow or lashed by winter gales, but keeps its columnar shape well. As a soft grey foil to the Purple Dawyck beech, and as a focus of interest during the winter months, this conifer has few equals.

Robinia pseudoacacia Bessoniana forms a reliably compact, rounded crown shape that will not approach the height usual for the false acacia, and it is usually without the prickles that sometimes make the

143

full-sized tree unpopular. *R. pseudoacacia* itself, a native of the eastern USA, has been growing and flourishing in Europe, including Britain, for well over three centuries, well known for its capacity to survive and thrive in poor soils and industrially polluted areas—a hardy resilience which Bessoniana shares. The fragrant white flowers in drooping clusters—readily distinguishable from the yellow, miniature powder puffs of the true acacias—are framed in June by the light green, almost fern-like foliage, and the contrastingly dark and rugged bark of the crown branches.

Also with fragrant white flowers in June and July, but a large and shapely bush rather than a tree, to balance the V-formation of this group is *Chionanthus virginicus,* the fringe tree—well known on the eastern side of North America, and well adapted to British conditions, having been grown successfully in England since early in the eighteenth century. The fascinating fringed flowers are followed by blue-black, sloe-like fruits in the autumn, and the spreading branches with their large, oblong-pointed leaves give balance to the tiered dogwood at the farther end of the arrangement. Like the others in this group, the fringe tree thrives in most soils and enjoys a sunny site.

Pink flowers and foliage will bring out the striking blends of colour in the group—whether this colour derives from shrubs, herbaceous plants or bedders. A climber such as *Clematis montana rubens,* with its glorious spring floral display, can have a stunning impact. It is not a plant that may be allowed to scramble freely over the tree foliage, but there is no reason why it should not be placed so as to sprawl at ground level. Alternatively, if the V-formation of this plan has been used to enclose a garden shed or similar small structure, the clematis can be grown to cover this, and be seen through the tree stems.

A group for blossom and berry

From left to right: *Elaeagnus* × *ebbingei*
Sorbus americana
Sorbus meliosmifolia
Laburnum alpinum
Crataegus crus-galli Pyracanthifolia

This is a collection of tough subjects that will withstand any amount of exposure, and will thrive in all types of garden soil. As with the first group in Plan 12, which contains an evergreen *Elaeagnus,* the arrangement can be reversed if required to provide the best sheltering effect.

Elaeagnus × *ebbingei* is a vigorous, fast growing evergreen shrub of hybrid origin, very ornamental with its large leaves, green above and silver beneath, and attractive at close quarters with inconspicuous but fragrant flowers in the autumn and orange berries in the spring.

The first of the group to flower, with broad clusters of white flowers in May, is the Chinese whitebeam *Sorbus meliosmifolia,* one of the first *Sorbus* trees to open its buds in the spring. The American mountain ash *S. americana* is next to display its white blossom in late May, closely followed by the American *Crataegus crus-galli* Pyracanthifolia with typical white hawthorn blossom. The main flowering display finally closes with the so-called Scotch laburnum, *Laburnum alpinum,* which produces its beautiful golden chain flowers in June.

Following the spring berries of the *Elaeagnus,* fruiting of the other trees in the late summer and autumn results in a colourful scene, too, with the bright red clusters of the American mountain ash, the large reddish brown marbles of the Chinese whitebeam, and the crimson haws of the thorn. The laburnum does not berry, of course, but it is arrayed at this season with numerous pendulous pods, yellowish brown and quite conspicuous after the leaves have fallen.

The Asian tree in this group, *Sorbus meliosmifolia,* will tolerate a wide range of soil types and climatic extremes, and is known to resist the effects of industrial pollution. It has fairly large bright green leaves covering a crown of dark, purplish branches which are vivid enough, during the bare winter months, to make it stand out distinctively as a rigid little spire.

The American mountain ash, *S. americana,* occurs as a wild tree in Canada from Newfoundland to Manitoba, and it may be found in any protected pocket of indigenous hardwood forest from Minnesota to New York, and from there south along the Appalachian Mountain Range. It is also planted very widely both in gardens and as a street tree in the USA, and thrives in all types of soil. In many ways it is similar to the British mountain ash, but more spire-like in silhouette, with neatly upright branches. The fine foliage colours brightly in the autumn before falling for the winter.

Crataegus crus-galli is a hawthorn native to a wide range within eastern and central North America, where it is known as the cockspur thorn—a description of its long, curved spines. The narrow-leaved variety *C. c.* Pyracanthifolia, on the other hand, is without thorns, and is one of the most remarkably shaped little trees, with a densely twiggy but amazingly symmetrical spreading umbrella shape, which develops as the tree matures. It is able to grow on unpromising sites in a wide

145

variety of poor soils and, though it might not be readily obtainable, any garden owner interested in the unusual would find it worthwhile to make enquiries of the larger tree-growing firms, for the unique shape of *C. c.* Pyracanthifolia could be used in many small garden designs.

Laburnum alpinum, the Scotch laburnum, is actually a southern European native that was introduced into Britain as long ago as the sixteenth century. It grows into a picturesque little tree, more compact than the common laburnum, and with larger flower clusters.

The pendulous laburnum flowers will be enhanced, and the whole group distinguished with a touch of luxury, if a climbing wisteria is planted inside the V-formation, clear of the tree roots, and trained into the lowest branches of the American mountain ash, from there to spread out over the other trees. Once well developed, its magnificent flush of flowers in June will create a charming effect, and its twining stems will slowly weld the group into a solid screen. It can easily be curtailed if any part of it threatens to damage the smaller trees, and it may be pruned hard back twice a year to improve its flowering performance.

With the accent on pink and red

From left to right: *Acer sieboldianum*
                       Embothrium coccineum lanceolatum
                       Acer palmatum Senkaki
                       Parrotiopsis jacquemontiana
                       Staphylea holocarpa Rosea

This is a woodland group, and the soil should be loamy and moist, preferably on the acid side, with plenty of humus material. Side shade is beneficial, and there would be no objection to light overhead shading from very tall trees. An open, sunny garden would also support this selection, but the site should be sheltered from cold winds.

Two maples of contrasting silhouette have been used in this arrangement, both natives of Japan. *Acer sieboldianum*, with its neatly rounded crown, is not one of the hardiest of the genus, but it does well in southern Britain at least, and the more southerly of the United States. It can be grown in colder areas provided the site is well sheltered. This is quite an attractive tree in the spring when decorated

(Opposite) Laburnum alpinum. The so-called Scotch laburnum—a southern European tree—produces its beautiful golden chain flowers in June

147

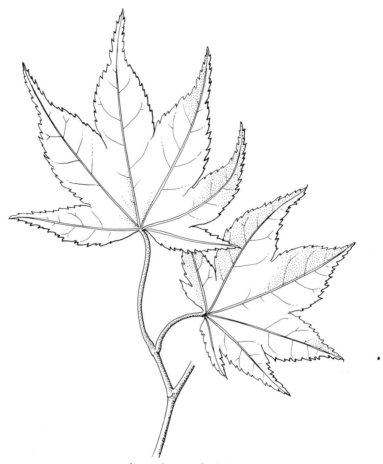

Acer palmatum Senkaki

with dainty clusters of yellow flowers, and later in the year with its bunches of wide-splayed keys. The finely toothed leaves colour a rich, deep red in the autumn. The other maple of the group, *A. palmatum* Senkaki, carries this red tone through the winter, for all its shoots and young branches are a conspicuous coral pink—from a distance, a warm pastel shade—which makes it a striking sight when the tree is bare. Most of the Japanese *palmatum* maples are bushy and shrub-like, but Senkaki, which has sometimes been called the coral bark maple on account of its bark colour, makes a fine little tree. Handsome in foliage too, with its large, deeply lobed leaves, *A. p.* Senkaki takes on a contrasting yellow tone for the autumn.

In the spring, clusters of pink flowers appear along the gracefully

148

A small, spreading tree, *Staphylea holocarpa* Rosea has no objection to high overhead shade. The flowers are pink

spreading branches of *Staphylea holocarpa* Rosea, and the small, compound leaves also have a bronzy-pink tinge as they open and expand. The species itself was introduced from China early in the twentieth century, and the pink variety Rosea has appeared as a garden tree since its introduction. It is a true woodlander which has no objection to overshading by tall trees, and it will succeed in a wide range of soils.

Another true woodland tree or large shrub which revels in shady, moist, peaty conditions, is the Himalayan *Parrotiopsis jacquemontiana*, somewhat similar to, but not as spreading as, the closely related *Parrotia persica*. It bears yellow-stamened white flowers from April to June, and the large rounded leaves colour brightly in the autumn.

149

Embothrium coccineum lanceolatum is the Norquinco Valley firebush from Chile, hardy in southern and western Britain at least, where it makes a neat little tree. In North America, it grows very well in the southern states, and luxuriates in the Mississippi Plains region. In colder areas it needs a well-sheltered site—another true woodland native which hankers after a moist, loamy soil, rich in humus but free from lime. Firebush is one of the showiest of plants in May and June when covered with brilliant scarlet blooms and, though rarely evergreen during British winters, it will keep its leaves the year round in milder climates.

The red and pink theme so much to the fore in this selection could be continued at ground level by making full use of red-flowering herbs and shrubs, concentrating on the darker crimson shades so as not to distract the attention too sharply from the charm of the trees themselves. A possible choice is the June-flowering deep crimson *Paeonia officinalis* Rubra Plena, followed in late summer, perhaps, by the crimson *Astilbe* Fanal.

Plan 13
Groups of four, spreading to a total width of 17m (56ft)

A compact arrangement of contrastingly shaped crowns, not intended to form a solid screen near ground level. The planted area will appear larger than it actually is. Measurements on the ground are 11.75m (39ft) by 5m (16ft).

A selection of flowering cherries

From left to right: *Prunus pseudocerasus* Cantabrigiensis
                             Prunus subhirtella Stellata
                             Prunus Snow Goose
                             Prunus Horinji
This selection is for a sunny garden with any ordinary soil.

First of the two rounded-crown forms in this group is provided by a variety of the Chinese cherry *Prunus pseudocerasus*, itself a white-flowered tree which opens its buds in March. Cantabrigiensis, as its name implies, is a Cambridge graduate, for it was raised in the

(Opposite above) The Judas tree, *Cercis siliquastrum*, is spectacular when the blossom opens in May and handsome in full leaf throughout the summer

(Opposite below) Gleditsia triacanthos Sunburst—a small, yellow-leaved variety of the North American honey locust

Cambridge University Botanic Garden about the time of World War I, and achieved an award of garden merit for its performance there. It differs from the parent species in producing pink blossom in sweetly fragrant clusters as early as mid February, so that it qualifies as a winter rather than a spring-flowering tree. In silhouette, *P. p.* Cantabrigiensis is not strictly symmetrical, and the crown is less dense than many cherries, but it has an informal beauty of its own.

The second rounded-crown member of the group, Snow Goose, is far more symmetrical, its upward slanting branches forming a dense, twiggy sphere that balances perfectly the somewhat gaunt shapes of the other trees. It flowers some two months later than *P. p.* Cantabrigiensis but, even so, the foliage buds have only just started to open as Snow Goose comes into full bloom. Its imaginative name well describes the dense texture and rotund form of this neat little tree during April when it becomes laden with pure white blossom, like the down-feathered breast of some exotic bird. *Prunus* Snow Goose originated as a hybrid between two ancient Japanese garden cherries: Fuji, a favourite subject for the traditional Japanese tree-dwarfing art of bonsai; and Oshima, an ancestor of many modern flowering cherry trees.

Fan-shaped crowns in this selection are seen in *P. subhirtella* Stellata, and in the hybrid Horinji. The Japanese spring cherry *P. subhirtella* is a very variable tree with rather small flowers, and the variety Stellata is a greatly improved form of the species—a hardy little tree of great informal beauty, its high-ranging branches laden from the end of March through much of April with clusters of large, pink, star-shaped flowers.

P. Horinji descended from the wild hill cherry of China and Japan, and is one of the most useful as a solitary specimen tree for a small garden, with its wild, untrained appearance, but reliably restrained dimensions. The flowers appear just as the bronzy young foliage is unfurling in April—semi-double blossom of a soft lilac-pink, each flower framed with dark reddish puce—a setting which brings out the delicate colour in high relief.

The high-branching habit of these trees will allow bulky shrubs to be planted beneath and around them, if the intention is to provide a solid shelter. Evergreens such as the beautiful gold and silver variegated *Elaeagnus pungens* Maculata, the silvery green *E. macrophylla*, and the hybrid *E.* × *ebbingei*, with a bright silver reverse

(Opposite) An effective small group dominated by *Acer palmatum* Senkaki, the coral bark maple

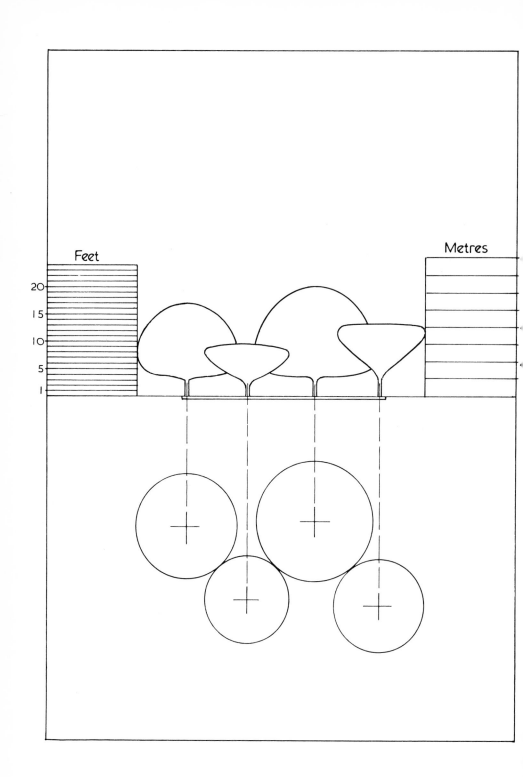

Feet

Metres

20
15
10
5
1

to its dark green leaves, will soon grow and bush out to make an impenetrable, peep-proof screen.

A long season of colour

From left to right: *Crataegus tomentosa*

Prunus serrula

Crataegus ellwangerana

Malus halliana Parkmanii

These tough little trees will grow in any type of soil under normal garden conditions, provided they are not too heavily shaded, and would do well in grimy industrial situations.

The twin dome shapes in this selection are provided by two North American hawthorns. The larger of the two, *Crataegus ellwangerana*, has a very wide natural range over Canada and the USA, and has proved completely hardy in Europe and Britain since its introduction at the turn of the twentieth century. It is very similar to the wild British *C. monogyna* in the white blossom which appears early in June, but it makes a smaller tree, and has noticeably larger, more rounded leaves, and extra large, bright red berries.

C. tomentosa also has a very extensive native range over much of Canada and the eastern and central USA, and was introduced to Europe as early as the mid eighteenth century. It is a conspicuous little tree when in bloom at the end of May, its neat shape heavily laden with white blossom, later to develop into strikingly large and unusually shaped amber berries. It is conspicuous, too, in the autumn when the downy foliage takes on bright colours before falling.

If the hawthorns represent solid respectability, the other two members of the group add a touch of spirited elegance. The little Chinese cherry *Prunus serrula* has dainty, willow-like foliage which matches perfectly its bright reddish-brown peeling bark. The small white flowers which cluster along the branches during late April are not so eye-catching as those of the Japanese cherry hybrids, but their small size does not detract from the year-round charm of this vigorous little tree.

Its matching partner is one of the most ornamental crabapples, with its high arching branches, its neat, glossy, dark green foliage, and, in early May, the rose-pink blossom in drooping clusters, each semi-double flower displayed on a red stalk, to be followed later in the year

Plan 13—Groups of four trees, spreading to a total width of 17m (56ft)

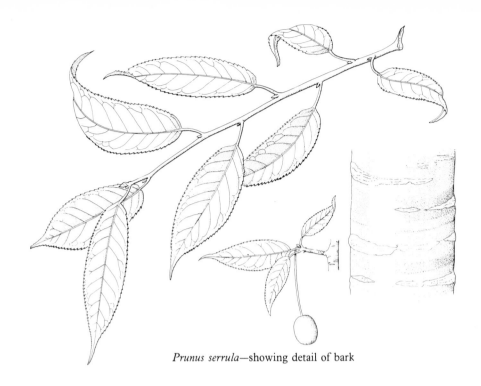

Prunus serrula—showing detail of bark

by purple berries. *Malus halliana* Parkmanii is a selected form of a Far Eastern species and able to grow in most soils and sites, both in America and Europe.

These little trees have the sort of sturdy build that could well be used to support climbing plants, to add interest with their festooning foliage and summer flowers. Such a plant is the sweetly scented white-flowered *Jasminum officinale*, which will scramble among the branches without doing damage and carry the flowering season through from June until the autumn.

Spring flowers and winter colour

From left to right: *Malus* × *atrosanguinea*
                        Corylopsis veitchiana
                        Prunus Kursar
                        Salix alba Vitellina

This unusual collection will thrive in an open, sunny situation in any reasonable type of soil. The trees are even more beautiful near a pond which can reflect the highlights of their colour whenever the sun shines during the winter and early spring, and the diversity of their shapes through the summer months.

156

Corylopsis veitchiana, a hardy little Chinese tree, has sweetly scented yellow flowers in April, clustered on neatly fan-shaped branches

A neatly symmetrical little tree to anchor the design, *Malus* × *astrosanguinea* is a hybrid between two Japanese crabapples which thrives happily wherever apples can be grown. It has bright glossy green foliage during the summer months, and is very attractive in blossom at the end of April and the beginning of May—the flowers are crimson in the bud, opening to a deep pink—to be followed later in the year by miniature red-cheeked apples.

The first spreading fan shape is provided by the Chinese shrubby tree, *Corylopsis veitchiana*, introduced to Britain during Queen Victoria's reign, and hardy enough to grow even on poor soils. Its garden value, apart from the neat silhouette and its tenacious ability to survive and thrive, lies in the handsome bright green foliage—two-toned with grey beneath the leaf—and the April display of sweetly scented yellow flowers in large clusters, each chalice-shaped bloom centred with contrasting, dark red anthers.

The larger tree with smoothly rounded contours is the hybrid flowering cherry, *Prunus* Kursar—a name which may sound Japanese in origin, but is formed from the first syllables of the two parent species: *P. kurilensis*, a Japanese shrub whose large flowers in April are white, tinged with a pink blush; and *P. sargentii*, a large, round-crowned Japanese tree, whose single pink flowers open in March. In late March and early April, Kursar becomes absolutely laden with bright pink blossom, in a wonderful combination of colour with the bronzed, yellowish green of the young foliage, which is opening at the same time.

A second fan shape is obtained by using a special technique, for *Salix alba* Vitellina, the yellow-barked version of the wild white willow, if allowed to grow unchecked will make a rounded silhouette. For use in this group, Vitellina should be pollarded by cutting all the growths back to the base of the crown, leaving a clear stem of 1m (3ft), and this must be done every second year in March. In this way the vigorous, sturdy young shoots with their glorious orange-yellow bark are able to form a distinct, fan-like outline. *S. a.* Vitellina left uncoppiced, while less vivid in bark colour, is nevertheless a very attractive tree, with its narrow, silvery green leaves which rustle in every breeze. It is less vigorous than the typical *S. alba*, and may be planted quite close to buildings without danger of the roots drawing moisture from the sub-foundation clay—a hazard with many willow trees. To take its place in this design, when newly planted, *S. a.* Vitellina must be allowed to form a single stem, which is beheaded at about waist height, but, for smaller groups, or when required as a coppicing shrub in its own right, it can be cut back to ground level.

An unusual ground cover for this group can be provided by planting the old-fashioned rambler rose 'Albéric Barbier', allowing it to sprawl along the ground between the tree stems, or climb a little way up them if it wishes, for it is a rose that will survive a modicum of shade. An early flowerer, with its clusters of creamy white, semi-double flowers, yellow in the bud, and yellow centred when full blown, it will extend the spring season into June.

Plan 14
Groups of three, spreading to a total width of 18m (60ft)

These fan-shaped trees will allow herbaceous or shrub borders to be planted virtually beneath their crown canopies and, similarly, they may themselves be planted close to buildings and other features, or

Plan 14—Groups of three trees, spreading to a total width of 18m (60ft)

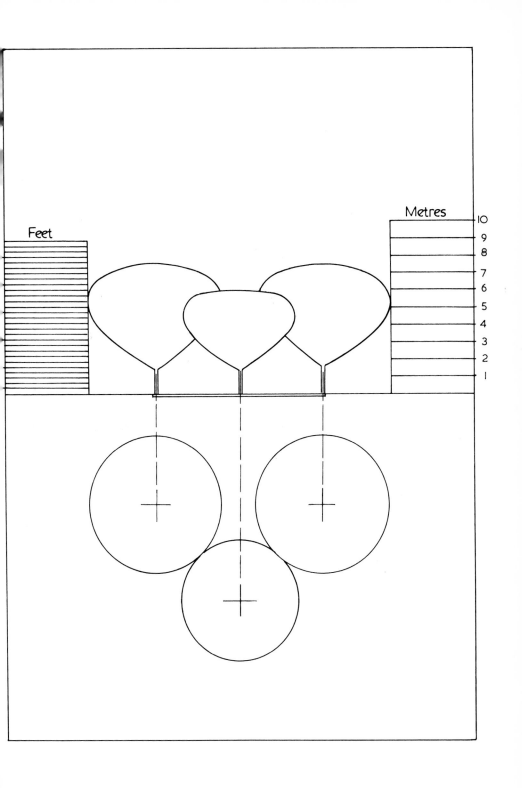

Feet

Metres

allowed to abut and overhang boundary walls and fences. The actual ground plan measures 10m (33ft) by 5.5m (18ft).

Spring flowering cherries

From left to right: *Prunus* Mikuruma-gaeshi
        Prunus Botan Zakura
        Prunus Pink Perfection

These cherries will grow in any type of soil, given a reasonably sunny site. As suggested below, the soil type may influence the choice of supporting plants.

The three trees in this group all flower in April, their blossom appearing just as the young leaves are opening with a metallic bronzy tinge—a colour which stresses each nuance of the variously tinted pink flowers.

Prunus Mikuruma-gaeshi is a somewhat gaunt tree with long, vigorous branches which become decked with a profusion of single, very pale pink flowers. *P.* Botan Zakura, the smallest of the three, is a graceful little tree, distinctive enough to be planted as an isolated specimen in a tiny garden, with comparatively very large semi-double flowers, which are pale pink and sweetly fragrant. *P.* Pink Perfection is said to be a hybrid between Kanzan, which features in the next group, and Shimidsu Sakura, which appeared under Plan 11, and, inevitably, it displays something of the characteristics of both. The pink double flowers are only slightly paler in tone than Kanzan, and hang in drooping clusters, usually lasting well into May.

With their distinctive, high-slanting branch structure, Mikuruma-gaeshi and Pink Perfection at least sometimes need curtailing and, with this in mind, all three are best considered as an inseparable group and allowed to intertwine, if they will. Their ascending branch angle often becomes less acute as the trees age, resulting in a broadening of the collective crown area, and it may become desirable to remove some of the lower limbs entirely. Whether these are lopped completely or merely shortened, the work is best carried out about July, and if any new buds start to expand and break leaf in the vicinity of the scar, these should be rubbed off before they have the chance to produce a cluster of unsightly twigs.

When planning supplementary planting around and beneath these cherries, one's choice will, of course, be governed by circumstances. Evergreen cover might be required for year-round shelter and privacy; flowering colour might be desirable during high summer; or a

Prunus Mikuruma-gaeshi

spectacular display may be planned to coincide with the flowering of the trees. If the soil is peaty and acid, some of the rhododendrons could be used to make spring a memorable season. Crimson is a colour that blends well with pink—the combination seems to stress the brilliance of the one and the purity of the other—and rhododendrons with flowers of this hue could be arranged, with the taller kinds at the rear of the trees and the smaller to the front. Tallest growing are the species *Rhododendron barbatum*, whose crimson flowers are dazzling in March, followed by the even brighter crimson in April of *R. thomsonii*. Among the smaller hybrid rhododendrons, one might choose the April flowering Elizabeth in dark red, and the May flowering Britannia in bright crimson.

161

Combining winter and spring flowering

From left to right: *Prunus* × *hillieri*
                               Cornus mas
                               Prunus Kanzan

Any garden soil will suit these hardy trees, and full sun is best, though they will have no objection to light shade from tall neighbouring trees.

Prunus × *hillieri*, a hybrid between the Fuji cherry *P. incisa* and the beautiful *P. sargentii*, is one of the most spectacular of the flowering cherries during April and May, when covered with a mantle of pink blossom. The broad crown is distinctive in silhouette, more bulky than Kanzan, and sometimes liable to spread in middle age. *P.* Kanzan is probably the best known of the Japanese cherries, certainly one of the most vigorous and, despite its size, more often planted in gardens than any other *Prunus* variety. It is certainly greatly to be admired every April when the stiff branches are completely covered with heavy, double blossom in a rich shade of mauvish pink, and it is used very frequently as a street tree—a role for which it is admirably suited. Like *P.* × *hillieri*, the crown tends to broaden as the tree ages, a tendency which can be countered by removing the largest lower limbs as necessary to keep it within bounds. When this is done, Kanzan tends to develop height at the expense of width. Pruning should be carried out always with an eye to retaining as narrow as possible a V-shaped outline and, as before, the best time to do this work is mid to late summer. Winter pruning is perfectly safe, but it often stimulates excessive twiggy growth which can mar the appearance of a tree if allowed to get out of hand.

Cornus mas is the so-called Cornelian cherry, a hardy southern European species of dogwood. It produces its tiny but prolific yellow flowers in late winter and early spring—a welcome touch of colour at this season—and these flowers are followed later in the year by edible, cherry-like fruits. Crimson tints usually colour the foliage during the autumn, and there are several varieties with coloured or variegated leaves to add brightness to the summer months. Cornelian cherry is often seen as a spreading shrub but, if at all encouraged, it will make the densely crowned, fan-shaped tree that this arrangement requires.

A woodland atmosphere can be invoked by careful choice of supporting plants set to grow around the tree stems, and spire-like flowers will dramatise the sparse, somewhat gaunt limbs of the tree crowns. Foxgloves will do this with their summer flowers in rich purple and white, and, if the ground beneath is lightly cultivated in

162

Cornus mas, the Cornelian cherry from southern Europe, produces its yellow flowers in late winter and early spring

late summer, they will seed themselves freely, and establish a colony between the trees.

Superb flowers and striking foliage

From left to right: *Magnolia* × *soulangiana* Rustica Rubra
                          Xanthoceras sorbifolium
                          Magnolia × *soulangiana* Lennei

A woodland type of environment is right for this selection, although they are perfectly hardy trees and will tolerate industrial site conditions and exhaust fumes near busy main roads. They will do best if the soil is slightly acid—quite heavy clay is suitable, and so are light, sandy soils, provided they have an addition of leaf mould, stable manure, or peat.

Magnolia × *soulangiana* is an old garden hybrid derived from two Chinese magnolia species, and it is one of the freest flowering magnolias suitable for gardens in the British Isles and the central and eastern United States. One of its most valuable assets is a willingness to flower while still young, for some magnolias need to grow for many years before they are able to develop flower buds. The two varieties

163

Xanthoceras sorbifolium, a Chinese mountain species able to grow in all types of soil, is hardy in Britain and much of North America

included in this group complement each other perfectly—a matching pair, and two of the finest and most reliable of the genus. Rustica Rubra has broad, cup-shaped, thick petalled flowers of a deep rosy red, and Lennei has creamy-purple flowers of the same type, opening during April and May while the large, rounded, dark green leaves are still expanding from the bud. As a bonus, they often produce a second batch of flowers in the autumn.

Xanthoceras sorbifolium is also Chinese, a handsome little tree with curl-pointed leaflets and May flowers in broad spikes somewhat resembling those of a horse chestnut or buckeye—the petals white with a pink central blotch. A mountain species by nature, hardy in Britain and much of North America, and tolerant of all soil types, it especially approves of the peaty conditions enjoyed by the magnolias, and balances their exuberance with its informal shape, refined flower spikes and neat little leaves.

(Opposite) Magnolia × *soulangiana* Rustica Rubra

Peat-loving ground-cover plants, allowed to run where they will around the stems, will help to conserve moisture in the soil and prevent vigorous weed development. Suitable plants are the spring-flowering lily of the valley, and its pink variety, *Convallaria majalis rosea*; the similar, also sweetly scented, white flowering *Maianthemum bifolium*; and, to follow, the evergreen *Galax urceolata*, which produces its dainty little white flowers in June and July.

Flowers and autumn berries

From left to right: *Sorbus hupehensis*
Malus hupehensis
Malus prunifolia

Reliably hardy trees, these will grow on reasonably fertile soil in sunny gardens anywhere.

Sorbus hupehensis is a Chinese mountain ash which sports a distinctive tinge of purplish blue throughout the year, in the winter to be seen in the compactly twigged branches of the spreading crown and in the summer appearing in the foliage. This colour contrasts well with the clusters of faintly unpleasant-smelling white flowers at the end of May and the beginning of June, and, much later in the season, with the large, pendulous bunches of white berries that hang on the tree long after the fine foliage has turned a brilliant red and fallen for the winter. White berries, it seems, have less attraction for the birds than red and orange ones, for they escape being eaten until other sources of food have disappeared.

Malus hupehensis is a crabapple from the Far East, introduced to the West at the turn of the twentieth century. Both this tree and the neighbouring mountain ash were named in their specific epithets after the province of Hu-pei in east central China, but their natural range seems to be far wider than this would imply. *M. hupehensis* flowers in the early summer, later than almost any other crabapple. The very profuse blossom is pink in the bud, opening to white, and is followed in late summer and autumn by small, yellow fruits. There is also a wholly pink-flowered form called Rosea, equally widely acclaimed in European and American gardens, and this has a laxer, more spreading crown silhouette.

Another Far Eastern crabapple, *M. prunifolia* has been grown in Britain for close on two hundred years, and is always greatly admired in the spring—it flowers at least a month earlier than *M. hupehensis*—when it produces a good show of pale pink blossom, crimson before the buds are fully open. It is handsome in foliage too, with large, rounded, bright green leaves, decorated later in the year with little red apples. All three trees are by nature inhabitants of mountainous regions, a habitat which suits them for life in moist, cool climatic zones everywhere.

Small, fairly open-crowned trees such as these can often be made to support a climbing plant with wonderful effect, and one such climber which will add a splash of colour from July to September is *Clematis viticella* Royal Velours, with beautiful nodding flowers of a deep crimson-purple. Other similar varieties of *C. viticella* that flower in equally colourful profusion are Kermesina and Abundance, and all these will climb perhaps halfway up the crowns of the trees in this group, and festoon their lower limbs.

A beautiful group at all seasons

From left to right: *Acer capillipes*
                         Gleditsia triacanthos Sunburst
                         Acer henryi

A moderately protected woodland-type garden is best for this selection, though all three trees are tolerant of fairly poor, dryish soils. Their ornamental foliage appreciates the shelter afforded by tall trees growing nearby, but likes to be able to feel the sun in the afternoons.

In this group, *Gleditsia triacanthos* Sunburst, the yellow-leaved honey locust from the USA, associates happily with two Far Eastern maples: *Acer capillipes*, a handsome little tree from Japan that has been grown in Western gardens since the nineteenth century, and has proved itself hardy and tolerant of a wide range of soils, though it is most at home in a woodland site; and *Acer henryi*, a Chinese native, also hardy in Britain and much of North America, where it is able to grow in quite poor soils. Both maples are highly ornamental at all seasons, not least during winter, when the very neat shape of their crowns is enhanced by their distinctive, conspicuously striped bark. Springtime sees *A. capillipes* tinted bright pink in the young shoots and opening foliage—the large, three-lobed leaves turning green for the summer, but colourfully displayed on long red stalks. *A. henryi* is particularly striking in the spring when laden with clusters of yellow flowers, while its leaves, in three separate leaflets, open to a strong tinge of bronze. Both maples display vivid autumn leaf coloration.

The honey locust, *Gleditsia triacanthos*, has a natural range from western Pennsylvania to Minnesota, and southwards to Texas and

Alabama. It will also grow near the east coast of the USA and in southern and eastern Canada, and, since the close of the seventeenth century, has been planted very widely as a garden tree in Europe and Britain. During subsequent years it has shown itself tolerant of all kinds of dryish soil, and has often succeeded in areas of grim industrial pollution. If given the choice it would prefer a woodland site, and in fertile soils within its native range it makes a sizeable tree. The variety Sunburst is usually much smaller than the typical species and seldom exceeds the bounds of this group. G. t. Sunburst is one of the most useful little trees, with bright yellow foliage which is particularly vivid early in the summer and a glorious sight when a ray of sunlight can pick it out from the surrounding shadow. In the autumn, the long brown seed pods which decorate the branches are very ornamental too, and the twigs and stem lack the fierce spines which arm the typical honey locust.

This is a lovely little woodland garden group, which looks all the better for an accompaniment of dark evergreen plants, with perhaps a touch of purple in flower or foliage. As a permanent framework of ground cover, the periwinkle *Vinca major* could be allowed to establish itself beneath the canopy, its purple flowers, when seen in close-up, accenting the coloration, sometimes subtle, sometimes bright, of the expanding tree leaves.

Plan 15
Groups of three, spreading to a total width of 19m (62ft)

This is the maximum branch spread that can be accommodated in a small garden, and the low branching habit of the trees in these groups prevents their being planted hard against a boundary fence, though the actual ground required measures only 9.75m (32ft) by 7.75m (26ft).

Subtle spring blossom and dramatic foliage

From left to right: *Prunus* Ukon
       Prunus incisa
       Prunus serrulata
Any type of soil will support these hardy trees, in any reasonably open, sunny site.

This selection is quite outside the usual run of flowering cherries,

Plan 15—Groups of three trees, spreading to a total width of 19m (62ft)

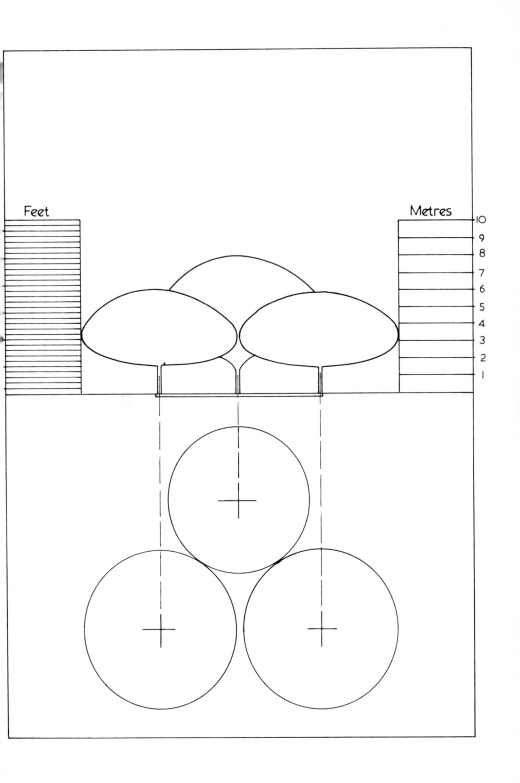

Feet

Metres

10
9
8
7
6
5
4
3
2
1

and there is no hint of the vulgarity many people see in the exaggeratedly heavy blossom produced by some Japanese cherry varieties. Instead, the spring display from March to May is one of subtle, delicate beauty.

First to flower is the Fuji cherry *Prunus incisa*, well known in British and American gardens since its introduction from Japan early in the twentieth century. Typically a very pretty little tree which becomes well covered with blossom during March, pink in the bud opening to pure white, there are a few popular varieties of the species which are similar in appearance but produce their flowers earlier in the year, such as February Pink, and Praecox, a winter-flowering form. If it is allowed to branch close to the ground, Fuji cherry can be grown as a large, bushy shrub instead of a standard or half-standard tree, with evenly disposed leaves from ground level, and this is the best form to adopt if a screen up to about 5m (16ft) high is needed.

Midway through April, *P.* Ukon starts to display its flowers in great profusion. They are very unusual in their colour—a pale greenish yellow—which harmonises beautifully with the glossy, coppery bronze of the young, newly opening foliage.

A vigorous, if somewhat gaunt tree, Ukon is one of the many hybrids which are probably descended from the third member of this group, *P. serrulata*, whose double white blossom opens towards the end of April and lasts well into May. This is an ancient Japanese garden tree, itself believed to have descended from the wild Chinese hill cherry, and introduced to the West early in the nineteenth century. Over the years, it has been used as a parent of the many flowering cherries to have been reared in Japan, Europe and America, hybrids which owe to this handsome tree much of their hardiness and ability to thrive in poor soils and uncomfortable sites.

Cherry foliage, after the delicate tints of spring, has a healthy, dark green appearance during the summer months, finally taking on the typical amber and russet glows of autumn. Ukon in particular becomes very richly tinted with orange and scarlet at this season. But, if weather conditions are harsh, or rainfall is short, the green foliage of high summer sometimes displays premature tints of scarlet and rufous yellow. The interesting colours, the shape and the texture of cherry leaves can be dramatised by setting an appropriate associate plant to cover the ground, climb the stems and clothe the branches as it twines through the crowns. The most striking plant for this purpose is the giant vine, *Vitis coignetiae*, itself a native of Japan, whose huge rounded leaves, up to 30cm (12in) across, are dark green on their upper surfaces and rusty brown beneath, colouring vividly during the autumn, in true vine tradition, with shades of crimson, scarlet and orange.

Magnificent blossom and contrasting foliage

From left to right: *Magnolia* × *veitchii*
 Prunus Ichiyo
 Catalpa bignonioides

A sheltered and reasonably frost-free garden with a fertile, moist soil is needed for this group and, for the sake of the magnolia, it should be free from lime. The other two trees will grow both in acid and alkaline soils, if they are to be planted as individual specimens, but the catalpa will still need a sheltered site, for high winds quickly damage its large, soft leaves.

Magnolia × *veitchii* is a hybrid between two Asian magnolias, *M. campbellii*, the Himalayan pink tulip tree, and *M. denudata*, the yulan lily tree from China. It is one of the most vigorous and ornamental trees of the genus, with its picturesquely spreading crown, and an amazing display of 15cm (6in) wide, bright, deep pink flowers in the spring. Like most magnolias, *M.* × *veitchii* does not produce its flowers until it is several years old and some 2m (6ft) high, but, once started, it breaks all records. A sizeable specimen can carry hundreds of flowers in April, covering the naked branches with a mantle of colour. It has a dark, handsome appearance in leaf, too, with purplish shoots and large purplish green leaves.

Prunus Ichiyo, one of the Chinese hill cherry group, is a vigorous tree whose wide-arching branches bear drooping clusters of strangely delicate double blossom of the palest blush pink. Towards the end of April, this frilled display corresponds with the breaking of the leaf buds and the unfurling of the bronzy young foliage.

Catalpa bignonioides is a magnificent tree. It comes from the eastern USA where it is known as the Indian bean tree, and it grows well in Britain. With its huge heart-shaped leaves, its spikes of foxglove-like flowers in July and August—basically white, with purple and yellow markings to be seen in close-up—and the spectacular pods up to 35cm (14in) long, which festoon the wide-spreading branches during late summer and autumn, this is one of the best specimen trees; one that will need careful thought before placing in a small garden, but which deserves to be included wherever space is no problem. The yellow-leaved variety Aurea is also a very fine tree, which is included in

Catalpa bignonioides, the Indian bean tree from the eastern USA, grows well in Britain but needs careful placing to accommodate the wide-spreading crown. The blossom is white with purple and yellow markings

another selection for this planting arrangement.

Few plants will thrive in the rather dry shade beneath these heavily leafy trees. Once they are well established, so that there is no root competition, the area below the branch spread could be planted with the brightly variegated *Luzula maxima* Variegata, a close-growing, grass-like giant woodrush about 50cm (20in) high, its glossy, light green and cream stripes in strong contrast with the broad, dark green leaves of the tree canopy overhead.

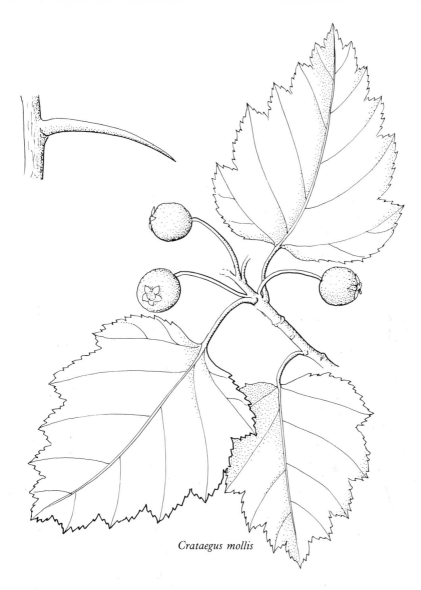

Crataegus mollis

Bright autumn fruits

From left to right: *Malus* Chilko
                     Crataegus mollis
                     Sorbus folgneri Lemon Drop

This is a collection of completely hardy trees that will flourish in an open, sunny site, even in poor soils or in areas subject to industrial pollution or highway exhaust fumes.

Selected for their brilliant fruits, these little trees are not without beauty of blossom too, and *Malus* Chilko puts on a wonderful display

173

of wine-red flowers in April. This broadly spreading crabapple, raised in Canada, has become a favourite garden tree, with its large flowers, its handsome foliage, and the miniature but edible crimson-skinned apples that develop in profusion during late summer and autumn.

Crataegus mollis, known in America as the red haw, is found wild in Canada and the central USA, and has often been planted in gardens for the sake of its sheets of white blossom, usually open by the end of May, and for the large, bright red berries which follow later in the season. The name *mollis* refers to the leaves, which are soft and downy. This is a thoroughly hardy hawthorn which can safely be planted wherever trees are able to grow, and is useful as a specimen tree for roadside areas poisoned by exhaust fumes.

Lemon Drop, a recently raised seedling of the Chinese whitebeam species *Sorbus folgneri*, is not lacking beauty in its white flower clusters which are on display in May, but it has been named to describe the bright yellow berries which hang along the branches in drooping clusters during late summer and autumn. Lemon Drop has pleasantly rounded leaves that are dark green on their upper surfaces and downy white beneath, and is one of the handsomest of whitebeams, with its spreading, almost weeping habit. The typical species *S. folgneri* has been grown in the West for a hundred years or more, and this clone has certainly inherited the hardiness and robust constitution of its parent.

For all their beautiful foliage, trees such as these are a little short of colour in midsummer, and if a shrub can be found that will share their site—however poor the soil or polluted the area—and produce a floral display to fill the gap between blossom and berry, it will complete the picture. One such shrub, from the eastern USA and Canada, is the suckering *Rosa nitida*, which makes a low, densely prickled thicket. It displays large, single, bright pink flowers in June and July, followed by scarlet hips, and is conspicuous among roses for the brilliance of its autumn foliage colours. With this combination, the season of leaf fall sees the red and yellow fruits displayed along arching branches, above a carpet of amber, scarlet, crimson and orange.

A woodland display of green and white

From left to right: *Amelanchier asiatica*
Acer monspessulanum
Cornus florida

For the best results, the garden should be moderately sheltered for this

Amelanchier asiatica

selection, with light overhead shade and a fertile, moist soil, preferably without lime. But these three trees are quite accommodating, and will grow in sunny sites, even when the soil is slightly alkaline.

There is no hint of gaudiness in this arrangement, but, nevertheless, it can be a dazzling sight in May when the juneberry and the dogwood are both in full flower. For the brief autumn season it can be breathtaking, with vivid crimson, scarlet and orange foliage tints.

The Chinese juneberry *Amelanchier asiatica* was introduced to the West from an area near the Yellow Sea midway through the nineteenth century; it is a truly graceful little tree, and tolerant of a wide range of sites and soils, though it will soon suffer during periods of drought. In the spring, numerous clusters of fragrant little white flowers appear as the leaves are expanding, soon followed by the black, currant-like juneberries.

Cornus florida is the flowering dogwood, native to the eastern and southern USA, and perfectly hardy in Britain. The foliage is quite attractive—the leaves in summer are a light green above, with a grey down on their undersides, while in autumn they match those of the *Amelanchier* in the brilliance of their orange and scarlet tints. In May, the tree produces large, cross-shaped white flower bracts, which make it quite strikingly conspicuous. There are several varieties which have been selected for the size or colour of their bracts, and Eddie's White Wonder, which has pure white, larger bracts carried on a similarly spreading, vigorous branch system, is a hybrid between this species and another American dogwood.

The upright member of this group is the Montpelier maple, *Acer monspessulanum* from southern Europe—in some ways the southern counterpart of the British field maple *A. campestre*, but it has a more symmetrical crown system and, when planted in Britain, it grows less vigorously. In April—to open the flowering season of the group, before the leaf buds break—the Montpelier maple produces clusters of fragrant little white flowers which develop, by the late summer, into bunches of reddish keys, their seed wings distinctively close-callipered. During the summer months, the foliage has a cool look, with the rather small three-lobed leaves a pleasantly glossy dark green on their upper surfaces, and greyish beneath.

The quiet green and white theme in this selection of trees could very tellingly be continued at ground level, with a generous use of ferns planted in the shadiest spots, and a selection of summer bedders with white flowers in the sunnier places: white petunias and *Lavatera* Mont Blanc, white-flowered hostas and peonies, wake robins and lilies.

A spectacular group

From left to right: *Catalpa bignonioides* Aurea
Paulownia tomentosa
Cornus florida Cherokee Chief

These beautiful trees need a sheltered garden with a good, deep soil. Though fully hardy in growth, frost may damage their flowers and high winds will tear the foliage. For the best visual effect, the group should be sited in front of a dark background to bring out the flower and leaf colour.

Like the typical green-leaved form of the Indian bean tree, *Catalpa bignonioides* Aurea is hardy over much of North America and also in Britain, where it grows well, especially if given a sheltered site with a loamy, well-drained soil. Exposure to high winds during the summer is to be avoided, because the huge, ornamental leaves are liable to tatter and turn brown at the edges. In the summer, like the species, Aurea bears charming clusters of white flowers with yellow and purple markings—but the spectacularly long, pendant pods which follow them are more conspicuous. *C. bignonioides* Aurea is one of the most beautiful yellow-foliaged trees, and it keeps its rich golden yellow colour well from spring to autumn, the huge, heart-shaped leaves soft and velvety to the touch—a truly dramatic tree.

In balance with the broad, spreading crown of the yellow Indian bean tree, the tiered branches of the red-flowered dogwood form a perfect match. The typical, white-flowered *Cornus florida*—the dogwood tree which featured in the preceding group—is an American native, and the best red and pink bracted forms have been selected in the USA from the naturally occurring variety *C. f. rubra*. Cherokee Chief displays gorgeous, cherry-red, cross-shaped blooms in May, and the variety Spring Song also has crimson bracts. The effect of these bright red flowers during the spring, as the foliage of the bean tree is expanding in amber and gold, is spectacular. Like the typical species, Cherokee Chief has two-tone light green and downy grey leaves, and the combined foliage colour and texture alone of these two trees, one on either side of the upright *Paulownia* with its huge, lobed leaves, make this group well worth the considerable amount of space needed.

Grown as an isolated specimen, the Chinese foxglove tree *Paulownia tomentosa* develops into a compact little tree, smaller, usually, than the other very similar members of its genus, *P. fargesii, P. fortunei* and *P. lilacina*. Its pale pinkish-purple spikes of foxglove-like flowers open in May, although the buds are already formed the previous autumn, and heavy frosts in the spring are apt to damage them. In a sheltered, sunny grove, however, there are few prettier sights when the petals are open and, apart from this risk of frost damage to the flower buds, it is a perfectly hardy tree in Britain and the eastern United States, thriving in any reasonably good soil.

The spreading silhouette of these three trees as a group will make the garden they occupy seem larger than it actually is, for they are not tall enough to dwarf adjacent buildings—a fate which is liable to overtake bungalows and chalet-style houses when sizeable trees are growing nearby. The miniature woodland atmosphere that these trees create will be enhanced if a drift of bluebells can carpet the ground, to flower before the tree foliage has fully opened, for the summer shade beneath the boughs is too dense for flowering plants, and the bluebells at this season will form a lush, green, weed-excluding cover.

Chapter 3

Specimen Trees in Isolation

In making the decision to plant an isolated specimen tree in the garden, which sort to choose, and precisely where to site it, the most important factor will be spatial: the proportions of such a tree in relation to the rest of the garden in plan and in profile, both at the time of planting and in the years to come.

Formal symmetry is often best avoided when choosing an isolated specimen tree; its effect may well be to create an optical illusion and exaggerate conditions in an unfortunate way. Thus, a strictly upright tree planted in a closely confined space, far from giving the impression of room to spare, tends to make the area seem even more cramped than it is. Fastigiate and columnar trees in isolation are therefore better sited in a comparatively large and open space where they can look majestic. Conversely, trees with spreading crowns, by their expansive appearance, introduce a hint of broad acres and make even a small plot seem spacious.

In plan, a substantial space should stretch uncluttered between the viewpoint and the isolated tree; this open space can itself be manipulated at will, and is no less a feature of garden design than the other planting arrangements—the lawn, the flower beds, and the composite groups of trees and shrubs. The 'isolation' of a specimen tree is not a term intended to imply a surrounding area where nothing taller than grass may grow. The tree will be quite as isolated in effect if it is situated at one extremity of a planting scheme, perhaps with fairly low ground-covering plants linking the two themes, and gradually building height into a border of shrubs.

In profile, whether in the grounds of a stately home or in a suburban plot, the isolated specimen tree no less than a composite group should be sited with an eye for the background—what it is destined to conceal or obscure, to stress or frame; every case will be different. The scale of the tree at its eventual maturity should be considered within the context of nearby composite groups of trees and shrubs. It should never happen that the impact of a large tree throws the other arrangements out of proportion. Very small trees, especially those with neat outlines, rarely harmonise but often clash with large forest trees. Subjects with very symmetrical, formal crowns rarely blend happily with purely informal types, and it is always safer to combine formal with semi-formal, or semi-formal with informal; in this way the more extreme features of contrasting but equally beautiful trees are allowed to blend gradually, and never create discord in the garden.

Most strictly formal trees are comparatively small—below 10m (33ft) in overall height—and most of them will feature in the descriptions of composite groups, and are listed in the summary. A typical formal tree of the larger size is the fastigiate hornbeam, *Carpinus betulus* Fastigiata. This makes a neat spire as a young tree, broadening on maturity into a solid cone, closely symmetrical, measuring about 15m (50ft) tall by 7m (23ft) across. The smaller variety *C. b.* Columnaris is slower growing, more symmetrical and very closely branched, not usually exceeding a height of 8m (26ft) and a spread of 3.5m (11ft).

Amongst conifers, the most glaringly formal of all is the monkey puzzle or Chile pine, *Araucaria araucana* which, with its leathery, spiny leaves on spidery branches and frankly exotic appearance, made a very popular feature in Victorian gardens. A mature specimen will attain 20m (65ft) or more but, to look its best, it needs a good moist soil and a clean, country atmosphere.

The great majority of conifers are semi-formal in appearance when grown in isolation. Some are semi-formal in their youth but utterly informal as they mature; the cedars and some of the pines will fall into this latter category.

Cedrus atlantica: The Atlas cedar from Algeria and Morocco; in gardens the form usually seen is *C. atlantica glauca*, the blue cedar, one of the most popular garden conifers, which has been planted very extensively since its introduction early in Queen Victoria's reign, although at 30m (100ft) tall, it will eventually outgrow the average garden. In the Atlas mountains the soil may be poor and dry, but the blue cedar does best in fertile, moist conditions. The weeping blue cedar, *C. atlantica* Glauca Pendula, in contrast with the wild Atlas cedar, must be classified as a semi-formal tree; slower growing and rarely exceeding 6m (20ft) in height, strongly weeping and very graceful, it is more suitable for the small garden.

Cedrus deodara: The deodar cedar has been grown in British and American gardens for generations, and makes a very graceful informally weeping tree. It takes up less room than the other wild cedars, though it still makes a massive tree up to 45m (150ft) tall. Even more than the Atlas cedar, the deodar needs a fertile, moist soil for healthy growth.

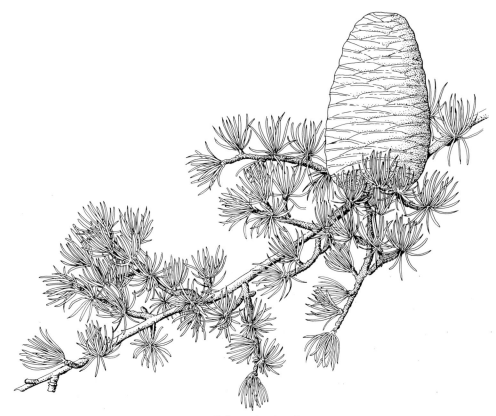

Cedrus atlantica glauca

Cedrus libani: The cedar of Lebanon has for centuries been associated with stately homes, and is known best as an aged tree, perhaps 25m (80ft) tall, with a heavy, flat-topped crown and wide-spreading limbs. In its youth, however, it forms a neat pyramid, and will retain this shape for several decades. As with the other cedars, though it will grow in poor conditions, a good fertile soil will ensure that it stays green and healthy.

Pinus nigra: The Austrian pine is a heavily branched, darkly sombre pine which makes a powerful specimen, especially suitable for poor, dryish soils. Its relative the Corsican pine, *P. nigra maritima*, is lighter both in colour and in branching habit, casts less shade, and grows well in poor, chalky or limy soils. Both trees can attain 40m (135ft) or more.

Pinus sylvestris: The Scots pine, a native of Britain and Europe, is symmetrically cone-shaped when young, but develops a picturesque, broadly spreading crown of heavy, orange-barked limbs as it matures. At maturity, by when it might have attained 30m (100ft) or more, it is one of the most beautiful informal specimen trees.

The bulk of the conifers remaining retain their semi-formal proportions even into old age. A selection of the best for garden use, in appearance and temperate climate hardiness, will include:

Calocedrus decurrens: The incense cedar is a native of the North American Pacific coast from Oregon south to Lower California, with more than one form in the wild. The name Columnaris is sometimes used to distinguish the familiar tower-like form that was introduced into Britain in the mid nineteenth century, eventually making a 30m (100ft) column of closely tiered fan-shaped sprays of dense, dark green foliage—in the USA it may top 45m (150ft). It prefers a good soil, a sheltered site, and clean air.

Chamaecyparis lawsoniana: The Lawson's cypress, from the Pacific coast forests of Oregon and California, grows very well in Britain where the wild species makes a beautiful specimen tree attaining a height of some 25m (80ft). Its numerous varieties are among the best known garden conifers, and include:

Allumii: One of the earliest Lawson's cypress cultivars to be introduced to gardens and still very popular. It will attain some 12m (40ft) eventually, but is very slow growing and retains its silhouette well as it matures. The dense spray-like foliage has a bluish tinge.

Columnaris: One of the most reliable of the columnar cultivars, reasonably quick growing, but seldom exceeding an overall height of 7m (23ft), and a span of 1m (3ft). It has upright, flattened sprays of greyish sea-green foliage.

Ellwoodii: One of the best known and most popular garden conifers, often thought of as a rock garden tree, although it will attain 3m (10ft) or more; the dense and prickly foliage is grey-green, becoming bluer during the winter. The yellow-tipped Ellwood's Gold is smaller and slower growing, with a neatly compact habit.

Erecta: A very well known cultivar that has been popular since the mid nineteenth century. It has a distinctive, pointed oval shape and fine, glossy, closely arranged foliage of a cheerfully bright green, but the lower stems tend to become bare as the tree ages, and it needs discreet wiring after a few years to prevent the multiple stems separating when weighed down by snow. Old specimens can reach a height of 15m (50ft) with a spread of 4.5m (15ft).

Fletcheri: A deservedly popular cultivar with very firm, slightly prickly foliage of the dense, juvenile type, greenish-grey, becoming

greyish-bronze during the winter. Rather slow growing, it produces a neat rounded-columnar shape which, although multi-stemmed beneath the thick foliage, resists snow damage and remains rigid. Old specimens have been known to attain 10m (33ft), but a typical Fletcheri of 6m (20ft) will have developed a basal spread of 2m (6ft).

Fraseri: Very similar to Allumii, but of a brighter green; it has an attractive conical shape, but needs wiring to avoid separation of the multiple stems during heavy snow falls.

Headfort: Capable of reaching 15m (50ft) eventually, but very slow growing, a typical specimen with a height of 5m (16ft) would measure some 4m (13ft) across the base; it forms a firm pyramid of gracefully drooping foliage which has a silvery glaucous sheen.

Kilmacurragh: A spectacular column up to 15m (50ft) with a spread of little more than 2.25m (7ft); its sharply ascending branches bear the typical dark green foliage, and its shape renders it immune from damage by wet snow.

Pembury Blue: A fine, silver-blue cultivar of a really striking colour, making a round-topped cone rather similar to, but smaller than, the typical species. It will reach 10m (33ft) with a basal spread of around 4m (13ft).

Pottenii: This cultivar looks like a dwarf tree when young, on account of its very fine, softly dense foliage of a rather glaucous sea-green, and it is often planted on rock gardens. Eventually, however, it will attain 12m (40ft) or more, with a spread of 3.5m (11ft). Multi-stemmed beneath the thick foliage, it is best discreetly wired against the possibility of snow and gale damage.

Winston Churchill: With a fine rich golden-yellow colour summer and winter, this fairly slow-growing and very compact cultivar makes a solid column of typical, but very dense, closely arranged sprays of foliage, eventually reaching 6m (20ft), with a spread of 2m (6ft).

Chamaecyparis nootkatensis: Nootka or yellow cypress is a native of the western North American forests. It was not discovered botanically until the close of the eighteenth century, and the variety Pendula was in cultivation by the second half of the nineteenth century. *C. n.* Pendula forms a broader pyramid than the typical yellow cypress and, with its graceful habit and weeping foliage, needs an isolated site to be fully appreciated. It grows readily in Britain on a variety of soils, including clay, and a typical thirty-year-old British

(Opposite) A very slow-growing conifer, *Chamaecyparis lawsoniana* Allumii retains its neat silhouette well as it matures

specimen was found to measure 6m (20ft) tall by 4m (13ft) across the base.

Chamaecyparis obtusa: The Hinoki cypress is valued as a timber producer in its native Japan. It was introduced to the West during the mid nineteenth century, and grows well on a variety of soils and sites, in Britain seldom attaining much more than 12m (40ft) in overall height, with a spread of some 10m (33ft) across the base of the crown. It has horizontally flattened sprays of dark, glossy green foliage, set off by the reddish brown, peeling bark. The variety Crippsii makes a similar cone of smaller proportions—about 7.5m (25ft) by 5m (16ft)—but with rich yellow foliage. The dwarf tree *C. o.* Nana Gracilis is very popular as a rock garden plant; dark green and compact with the sinuous appearance of a Japanese bonsai tree, it will eventually attain 3m (10ft) or more.

Chamaecyparis pisifera: Sawara cypress makes a large timber tree in its native Japan. In Britain, where it was introduced midway through the nineteenth century, it rarely attains more than 6m (20ft) in height, with a spread of 4.5m (15ft). The reddish bark peels in long strips, and the dark green foliage is prickly, each leaf an erect, long-pointed scale on the flattened, horizontal sprays. The Sawara varieties Filifera and Plumosa are smaller than the type, the former with long, drooping leaf sprays, the latter with soft, feathery, bright green foliage.

Cryptomeria japonica: The Japanese cedar has a natural range in the mountains of Japan and central China. It makes a very attractive 20m (65ft) cone with long, drooping sprays of rather prickly, bright green foliage, and reddish brown bark peeling in strips. It grows well in Britain and the temperate USA on all normal soils.

× *Cupressocyparis leylandii*: The Leyland cypress, usually seen as a hedger, makes a fine isolated specimen tree, eventually attaining fairly massive proportions and a height of 25m (80ft) or more. In general appearance it is not unlike a Lawson's cypress, but it is said to be one of the fastest-growing conifers—in Britain, at least. Castlewellan Gold is a golden-foliaged cultivar of Leyland cypress.

Cupressus glabra: The smooth Arizona cypress, with its natural range extending from central Arizona to northern Mexico, is a tree that prefers warm, dry situations; the conical form *C. g.* Pyramidalis is more accommodating than the type, however, and grows well elsewhere in the USA and in southern Britain. A picturesque tree with

(Opposite) The weeping yellow cypress, *Chamaecyparis nootkatensis* Pendula, needs an isolated site to be fully appreciated

dense blue foliage and reddish, peeling bark, it has become one of the most popular blue garden conifers since its introduction between the World Wars. As a rule, it will attain some 15m (50ft) in height, with a spread across the base of less than 5m (16ft).

Cupressus goveniana: The Gowen cypress from Monterey, California, was introduced into Britain midway through the nineteenth century. Attaining 15m (50ft) in Monterey but usually much smaller elsewhere, it needs a mild, moist area such as the south-west coast of Britain, as it is liable to succumb to cold winters. The dark green foliage is similar to that of *Chamaecyparis lawsoniana* Erecta, and in old specimens the branches arch over to present a characteristically domed outline.

Cupressus macrocarpa: Monterey cypress, restricted in its natural range to a tiny area of California, grows rapidly in any mild, moist climate and does well in the south and west of Britain. The variety Donard Gold is very shapely, with fine, dense foliage of a rich deep yellow, and an attractive feathery appearance. A typical well-grown specimen measuring 15m (50ft) tall will have attained a basal spread of about 6m (20ft). Similar in colour and texture, the variety Goldcrest makes a narrower cone, a 15m (50ft) specimen spreading to about 4.5m (15ft) at the base.

Cupressus sempervirens Stricta: The Mediterranean or Italian cypress is the cultivated, upright form of a wild species which is found throughout southern Europe and in Asia as far east as Pakistan. The truly wild form has a horizontal branch system and is very different in appearance. Young plants of *C. s.* Stricta may be damaged by cold weather, but the variety is hardy in southern England, where the Romans planted groves near their villas and the descendants of these early reminders of home are still growing; it also flourishes in south-western Scotland, and in the southern USA where it grows happily on poor, dry soils. Individual trees have been known to top 40m (135ft), but the average height is about 25m (80ft), with a spread across the crown of 5.5m (18ft).

Juniperus chinensis: The Chinese juniper varies greatly in the wild—its natural habitat ranges very widely throughout the Himalayas and the Chinese mountains—and since its introduction to the West midway through the eighteenth century, numerous distinct forms have been raised. The variety Aurea has attractive yellow foliage and is reliably columnar, attaining a height of 6m (20ft), with a spread across the base of 2.5m (8ft). The variety Fairview was raised just before the outbreak of World War II; it has bright green, prickly foliage, and a typical specimen would measure about 3m (10ft) in height and 75cm (30in) across the crown. Raised about the same time, the American variety Iowa tends to be bushy while small, but eventually produces a slender column of rather bluish green, a mature specimen reaching some 6m (20ft) in height with a spread of little more than 1.25m (4ft).

Juniperus communis Hibernica: The Irish juniper is a narrowly compact, slow-growing, upright form of the extremely variable common juniper, which has geographical races occurring over much of the northern hemisphere, from Canada and the USA, through Europe and Asia as far east as Japan. *J. c.* Hibernica eventually forms a silvery blue column of around 5m (16ft) with a spread of about 70cm (28in), but garden specimens are usually smaller. It is often multi-stemmed and these stems, though stiff, tend to separate when lashed by gales, and are best discreetly wired.

Juniperus virginiana Skyrocket: This remarkably narrow clone is derived from a wild seedling of the so-called pencil cedar—a variable tree, and by no means confined to Virginia as the specific name might suggest, but found over much of central and eastern USA as far north as Canada. Skyrocket has become a favourite in Britain where, since its introduction during the late 1940s, the oldest has attained about 6m (20ft) in height, with a basal spread of no more than 40cm (16in), but most garden specimens are much smaller.

Picea abies: The Norway spruce very often finds itself planted in British gardens, having served indoors as a Christmas tree. All the spruces make very beautiful solitary specimens, especially when their branches are allowed to sweep the ground, as they are among the most symmetrical of cone-shaped trees. Norway spruce has a wide natural range from the Pyrenees and the Swiss Alps in the south to the forests of Norway and Sweden in the north, and eastwards to Siberia where it grows beyond the Arctic circle. Before the last Great Ice Age, it grew in Britain too, and is now commonly planted in forestry plantations. It prefers a moist, acid soil and does well on clay, but will grow in poor, dry areas, albeit more slowly. The variety Pyramidata has a narrower, more compact outline, a typical specimen measuring 20m (65ft) in height with a basal spread approaching 4m (13ft).

Picea breweriana: Brewer's weeping spruce is often said to be the most beautiful of all conifers. A native of a limited area of mountain land in Oregon and northern California, it has been planted very widely as an ornamental specimen tree in Britain and elsewhere. It should always be given the space to develop its full potential and to be seen clearly, for the slender branches and weeping shoots are draped with long sprays of dark green foliage like the folds of a theatre curtain. A well grown tree of 15m (50ft) will have developed a spread of about 9m (30ft).

Picea omorika: The Serbian spruce is limited by nature to a limestone mountain region in Yugoslavia, and when introduced elsewhere it does well on chalk and limestone soils. In Britain it can be used when the soil is limy in place of Norway spruce, which it resembles in foliage and silhouette. The variety *P. o.* Pendula has an attractive silvery appearance caused by the pendulous shoots twisting to reveal their white undersides. A typical specimen of 18m (60ft) will have attained some 3.75m (12ft) across the base.

Picea pungens: The Colorado spruce is a large timber tree in North America, but when grown in Britain it makes only a small, densely crowned pyramid. *P. p. glauca* is the blue spruce, a 25m (80ft) tree with greyish blue-green foliage, and the variety Koster is an improved form of this—a popular small garden tree in Britain, with very prickly, dense, silvery blue foliage.

Picea smithiana: Smith's weeping spruce from the western Himalayas is similar in general appearance to Brewer's weeping spruce, but much narrower in outline and less dramatic in effect. When young, it is vulnerable to frost damage in Britain, but often makes a fine specimen tree once it has passed the dangerous age, and will attain a height of 20m (65ft) with a basal spread of about 6.5m (22ft).

Pinus cembra: The Arolla pine is a popular garden conifer in Britain, where it makes a densely symmetrical cone of stiff, dark green leaves, ultimately about 6m (20ft) high with a spread of something over 3m (10ft). In its native home of Siberia, and in the forests of central Europe, it sometimes attains 40m (135ft) or more.

Pinus peuce: The Macedonian pine from the Balkans, a slow-growing but very healthy tree, making a neat cone of dense, bright green foliage, is tolerant of poor acid conditions, but not suitable for limy soils. A typical mature specimen in Britain might measure 10m (33ft) in height with a basal spread of some 5m (16ft).

Pinus wallichiana: The Bhutan pine is a decorative tree from the Himalayas, reaching about 20m (65ft), with a broadly spreading, slightly drooping crown of grey-green leaves, remarkable for its long, pendulous cones. It needs a lime-free soil and an open site to do well.

Taxus baccata: The common yew of Britain and Europe has several garden varieties, some of which are useful in composite groups, like the upright Fastigiata and Fastigiata Aurea at about 5.5m (18ft) tall by 2m (6ft) broad. One of the best varieties for specimen planting is *T. b.* Elegantissima, a broad, upright, conical bush, 6m (20ft) by 6m (20ft), with bright golden-yellow foliage.

Thuja plicata: The western red cedar from the forests of western North America is a rather similar tree to Lawson's cypress, but with a stiffly upright leading shoot. One of the best varieties for specimen planting is *T. p.* Zebrina, which may eventually reach a height of 30m (100ft) or more, and measure 15m (50ft) across the crown—a perfect cone of dense foliage, basically bright green, but variegated with a creamy yellow which gives the tree a golden appearance.

Several broadleaf trees of completely informal appearance are distinctive, picturesque or compact enough to be of value as garden specimens. A selection might include:

Acer pseudoplatanus Brilliantissimum: One of the best small varieties of the European sycamore, it slowly attains a height of about 8m (26ft) compared with the 30m (100ft) of a typical sycamore, which grows far quicker. The young leaves of Brilliantissimum are bright pink as they open in the spring.

Aesculus × *carnea*: The red horse chestnut attains a height of about 15m (50ft), with an informally rotund crown and heavy leaves like those of the common horse chestnut, and rosy red flowers in May.

Aesculus hippocastanum: The common white horse chestnut makes a huge tree of 30m (100ft), with an equivalent spread across the inverted pudding bowl of a crown. A well loved tree in Britain, with five-fingered leaves and white flower spikes in May, followed by the familiar conkers.

Aesculus indica: The Indian horse chestnut is intermediate in size between the red and the white conker trees, reaching a height of about 18m (60ft). It has glossy foliage and pale pink flowers.

Ailanthus altissima: The tree of heaven makes a very distinctive specimen tree, with a narrowly conical crown up to 15m (50ft). It is very fast growing for the first few years of its life, after which it grows more slowly. The leaves are not unlike those of an ash.

Arbutus unedo: The strawberry tree is a native of southern Europe and also grows wild around Killarney in western Ireland; a handsome evergreen which reaches a height of 9m (30ft), it has white flowers in the late summer, followed by edible fruits, rather like round strawberries.

Liriodendron tulipifera

Betula pendula: The silver birch. Many of the birches make good specimen trees about 15m (50ft) tall, and often look better when two or three are grouped together. The strongly weeping variety Youngii is particularly suitable for mixed groups.

Fraxinus mariesii: The flowering ash is an attractive tree up to about 7m (23ft) in height, with clusters of creamy white flowers in June, followed by purplish seed keys.

Fraxinus ornus: The manna ash is smaller than the wild British ash, attaining about 18m (60ft), but with heavier foliage that casts rather more shade. It bears fragrant white flowers in May.

Laburnum × *watereri* Vossii: This hybrid laburnum eventually makes a broad fan shape about 6m (20ft) high. It produces its long golden chain flower clusters in June, and grows well in any garden soil.

Liquidambar styraciflua: The sweet gum, a narrowly pyramidal but informal tree, reaches a height of around 20m (65ft) and has rough corky grey bark and lobed maple-like leaves which colour brightly in the autumn. It dislikes lime, but grows well in sandy soils.

190

Liriodendron tulipifera: The tulip tree, broad crowned and fast growing up to 30m (100ft) high, with oddly shaped leaves and greenish yellow tulip-shaped flowers in June and July, grows well in most garden soils.

Robinia pseudoacacia: The false acacia makes a very beautiful tree if allowed to grow without over-shading, with graceful foliage and pendulous clusters of white flowers in June. A native of the eastern USA, naturalised in Europe, and planted very frequently in Britain, it is noted for its ability to thrive in poor soils and industrially polluted situations. It will attain 25m (83ft), but there is a much smaller and very popular variety known as Frisia, which has foliage of a rich golden yellow, and this is excellent as a small garden specimen tree, or a composite group member.

Tilia petiolaris: The weeping silver lime is one of the most beautiful of the lime genus. It makes a 20m (65ft) tree with a high domed crown fringed by long, pendulous branches. The leaves have a silvery-white reverse which gives the foliage a shimmering, silver appearance when riffled by the breeze.

By virtue of their distinctive outline or their striking leaf colour, many broadleaf trees fit into the category of 'semi-formal specimen tree'. A few of the most noteworthy are:

Acer platanoides Crimson King: One of several readily obtainable coloured leaf varieties of the Norway maple, it is an excellent semi-formal specimen tree. Fairly fast growing, with large lobed leaves of purple-red, it will eventually attain some 18m (60ft).

Eucalyptus dalrympleana: The eucalyptus or gum trees have a somewhat exotic appearance, and their positioning should be planned with care. *E. dalrympleana* is fast growing and very hardy, with evergreen leaves which are sometimes bronze, sometimes grey-green, and a dappled bark of green and white, becoming smoothly white as it ages. It usually attains around 12m (40ft) in Britain.

Eucalyptus gunnii: This gum tree attains about 18m (60ft) in Britain; a handsome tree, it has bark mottled in grey and green, and evergreen leaves which are rounded and strikingly blue when young, but on older branches are green, long, narrow and curved.

Fagus sylvatica Dawyck: The Dawyck beech is a very symmetrical tree, eventually growing to a height of about 20m (65ft), with a spread across the crown of about 5m (16ft). The purple-leaved fastigiate beech Purple Dawyck is unlikely to grow as large as this, and makes an excellent, colourful subject for grouping. In complete

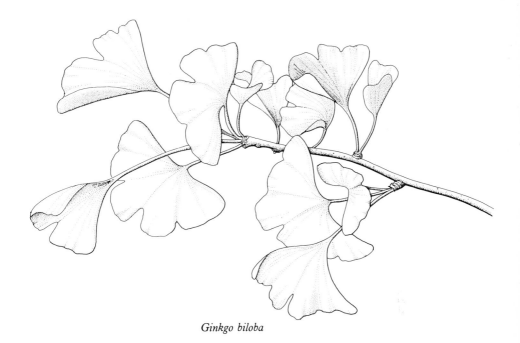

Ginkgo biloba

contrast is *F. s.* Purpurea Pendula, the weeping purple beech; not
too large or vigorous for garden use, and not casting so heavy a
shade as the wild type of beech, it rarely exceeds a height of 8m
(26ft). A splendid semi-formal weeper for siting as an isolated
specimen, it is useful as a backdrop of dark purple foliage.

Fraxinus excelsior Pendula: The weeping ash, smaller than the wild
   type, nevertheless makes a fairly large tree, eventually reaching
   some 20m (65ft) in height, with a spread across the crown of 15m
   (50ft).

Ginkgo biloba: The maidenhair tree, with distinctive fan-shaped leaves,
   has a conical crown. Its variety Fastigiata is narrowly columnar, and
   makes a striking specimen, eventually reaching 30m (100ft).

Ilex aquifolium: The wild holly of Britain and Europe—itself a useful
   small tree—has several variegated cultivars which can be grown as
   standard trees, and these have fairly rounded crowns. Eventually
   they will reach a height of 6m (20ft) and a span of 4.5m (15ft). The
   variety Argenteomarginata, the broad-leaved silver holly, has
   white-margined leaves and heavy crops of red berries; Argenteomarginata Pendula is the silver weeping holly, a charming little
   weeping tree with prickly white-margined leaves and a good crop of

(Opposite) Fagus sylvatica Purpurea Pendula, the weeping purple beech, is not too
large for garden use and provides a useful backdrop of dark foliage

berries; the hybrid *I.* x *altaclarensis* Golden King is an excellent variety with bright yellow leaf margins and also bears red berries.

Salix x *chrysocoma*: The golden weeping willow is one of the most popular garden trees, and consequently is often planted on sites far too small to accommodate it. In such places, and when grown as a member of a group, it needs careful summer pruning to keep it within bounds. As a free-growing specimen it will attain 18m (60ft) or more, with a comparable spread across the crown.

Plants which are normally grown as climbers or sprawlers sometimes make striking standard trees if given the appropriate treatment. Amongst them the wisteria and, on a smaller scale, the rambling roses are of outstanding value in garden design.

Wisteria floribunda: The Japanese wisteria is less vigorous than the Chinese species *W. sinensis*, and more suitable for use as a standard tree. It bears 20cm (8in) weeping clusters of fragrant bluish-violet flowers in May and June. The variety *W. f.* Macrobotrys (syn. *W. multijuga*) has paler lilac flowers which hang in clusters 1m (40in) or more long; *W. f.* Alba has white flowers in 50cm (20in) trusses. For the purpose of forming a standard tree, the young wisteria plant should be restricted to one sturdy shoot, securely tied upright to a stout stake which has a height above ground of at least 2.25m (7ft). The shoot should be cut at a suitable bud about 50cm (20in) above this point so that it branches out into a crown, and the first year or two of growth should be devoted to forming a good, symmetrical head of branches. Once this framework has been formed, annual pruning will entail removing the longest trails, and cutting back vigorous new shoots to their second bud during late summer.

Weeping standard roses: The rambling *Rosa wichuraiana* hybrids are best for this purpose, the criterion of choice being the quantity and timing of new wood to be produced each year. At the end of the first season all the shoots will need cutting back; thereafter only the wood which has flowered should be removed, cutting this out completely, preferably in the early autumn, leaving the newly produced rambling shoots intact to carry the following year's flowers. If these trails are inconveniently long, rather than being shortened, they can be tied discreetly to the base of the stake. If the growth during a poor season has not produced enough new wood, some of the old trails can be left, and the flower-bearing lateral shoots cut back to the first or second bud; they will flower again, though the flowers will be later and smaller than usual. Roses for weeping standards are best budded on a briar stock—the longer the better, for weeping standards need at least 1.5m (5ft) of clear stem to look their best. The stake will need to be 2m (6ft) long, and there should be at least two ties. Special wire umbrella-shaped frames have sometimes been recommended to support weeping standards, but these are cumbersome and unsightly. If appropriate rose varieties are used, artificial supports are quite unnecessary.

A list of the best varieties to use as weeping standards will include some of the oldest ramblers: Crimson Shower, slightly fragrant and very late flowering in crimson; Dorothy Perkins, an old favourite with rose-pink flowers; Evangeline, fragrant pale pink and white; Excelsa with fragrant crimson flowers; Lady Gay, with pink flowers; Lady Godiva, in very pale pink; and Minnehaha in very dark pink.

The early flowering, creamy white Albéric Barbier, and the salmon-pink Albertine, are among the most beautiful of ramblers and they are often grown in this style, but they seldom produce early annual growth that is clearly enough defined to make a perfect weeping standard, and pruning in their case will consist of trimming and thinning rather than the straightforward removal of long, rambling trails which have flowered evenly from stem to tip.

Chapter 4

Summary of Heights and Spreads

(Numbers refer to text page)

	Columnar		Conical	
	Height	Spread	Height	Spread
Acer capillipes, 167				
cappadocicum, 63				
× *coriaceum*, 84				
crataegifolium, 107				
davidii Ernest Wilson, 107			8m (26ft)	5m (16ft)
George Forrest, 106				
Madeline Spitta, 107	6m (20ft)	2m (6ft)		
ginnala, 139				
glabrum, 103				
grandidentatum, 84				
henryi, 167				
japonicum, 63				
Aureum, 107, 109				
Vitifolium, 91				
macrophyllum Seattle Sentinel, 84	8m (26ft)	3m (10ft)		
maximowiczii, 84			5m (16ft)	2.75m (9ft)
micranthum, 107				
monspessulanum, 174				
palmatum Dissectum Atropurpureum, 69				
Dissectum Flavescens, 53, 55				

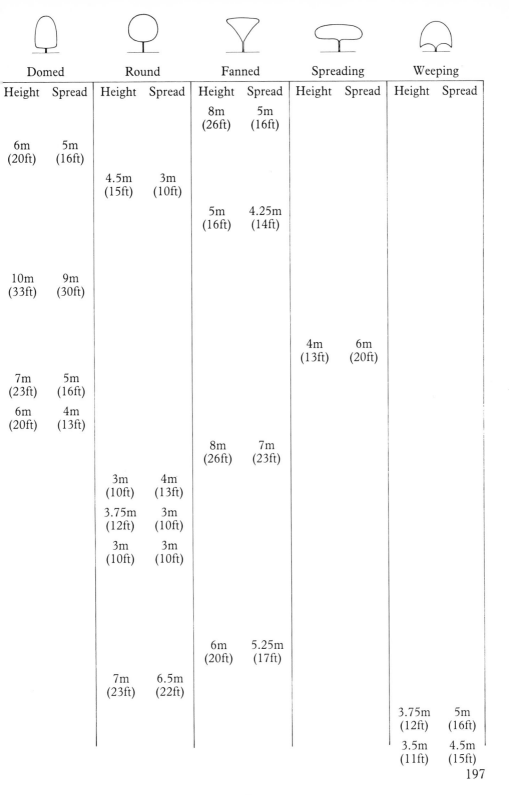

Domed		Round		Fanned		Spreading		Weeping	
Height	Spread	Height	Spread	Height	Spread	Height	Spread	Height	Spread
				8m (26ft)	5m (16ft)				
6m (20ft)	5m (16ft)								
		4.5m (15ft)	3m (10ft)						
				5m (16ft)	4.25m (14ft)				
10m (33ft)	9m (30ft)								
						4m (13ft)	6m (20ft)		
7m (23ft)	5m (16ft)								
6m (20ft)	4m (13ft)								
				8m (26ft)	7m (23ft)				
		3m (10ft)	4m (13ft)						
		3.75m (12ft)	3m (10ft)						
		3m (10ft)	3m (10ft)						
				6m (20ft)	5.25m (17ft)				
		7m (23ft)	6.5m (22ft)						
								3.75m (12ft)	5m (16ft)
								3.5m (11ft)	4.5m (15ft)

	Columnar		Conical	
	Height	Spread	Height	Spread
Acer palmatum Senkaki, 147, 152				
platanoides Globosum, 63				
rubrum Scanlon, 53	10m (33ft)	1.25m (4ft)		
Schlesingeri, 107			7m (23ft)	6m (20ft)
saccharum Temple's Upright, 63	7m (23ft)	2.5m (8ft)		
sieboldianum, 147				
Aesculus californica, 102				
× *carnea*, 189				
discolor, 35				
glabra, 102				
hippocastanum, 189				
indica, 189				
pavia, 91			7m (23ft)	4.5m (15ft)
Ailanthus altissima, 189			15m (50ft)	8m (26ft)
Amelanchier asiatica, 174				
florida, 139	7.5m (25ft)	3m (10ft)		
laevis, 111			9m (30ft)	5m (16ft)
Araucaria araucana, 179			20m (65ft)	12m (40ft)
Aucuba japonica, 15				

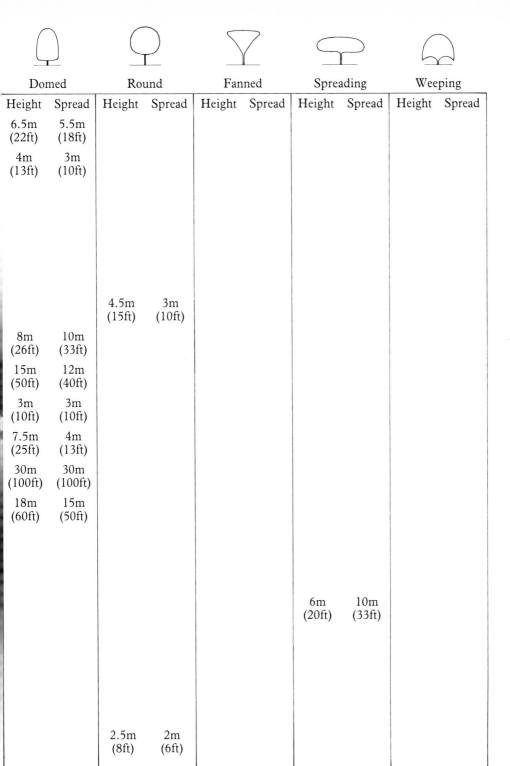

Domed		Round		Fanned		Spreading		Weeping	
Height	Spread	Height	Spread	Height	Spread	Height	Spread	Height	Spread
6.5m (22ft)	5.5m (18ft)								
4m (13ft)	3m (10ft)								
		4.5m (15ft)	3m (10ft)						
8m (26ft)	10m (33ft)								
15m (50ft)	12m (40ft)								
3m (10ft)	3m (10ft)								
7.5m (25ft)	4m (13ft)								
30m (100ft)	30m (100ft)								
18m (60ft)	15m (50ft)								
						6m (20ft)	10m (33ft)		
		2.5m (8ft)	2m (6ft)						

	Columnar		Conical	
	Height	Spread	Height	Spread
Berberis Barbarossa, 15				
Bountiful, 15				
darwinii, 15				
julianae, 15				
× *stenophylla*, 15				
wilsoniae, 15				
Betula pendula Youngii, 131, 190				
Buddleia alternifolia, 11, 15, 45				
davidii, 11, 15				
globosa, 15, 16				
Calocedrus decurrens, 181	30m (100ft)	5m (16ft)		
Camellia spp. and vars., 15				
Carpinus betulus Columnaris, 179			8m (26ft)	3.5m (11ft)
Fastigiata, 179			15m (50ft)	7m (23ft)
Catalpa bignonioides, 171, 172				
Aurea, 176				
Cedrus atlantica glauca, 179, 180			20m (65ft)	14m (46ft)
Glauca Pendula, 179				
Ceratostigma willmottianum, 15				
Cercidiphyllum magnificum, 69				

200

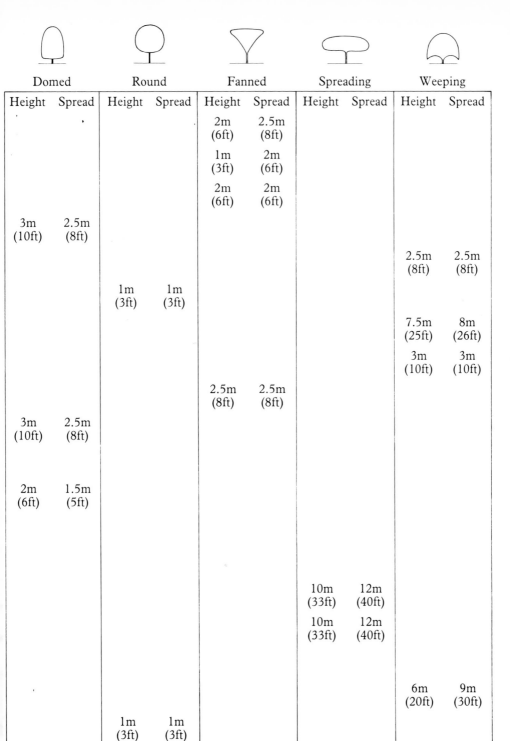

Domed		Round		Fanned		Spreading		Weeping	
Height	Spread	Height	Spread	Height	Spread	Height	Spread	Height	Spread
				2m (6ft)	2.5m (8ft)				
				1m (3ft)	2m (6ft)				
				2m (6ft)	2m (6ft)				
3m (10ft)	2.5m (8ft)								
								2.5m (8ft)	2.5m (8ft)
		1m (3ft)	1m (3ft)						
								7.5m (25ft)	8m (26ft)
								3m (10ft)	3m (10ft)
				2.5m (8ft)	2.5m (8ft)				
3m (10ft)	2.5m (8ft)								
2m (6ft)	1.5m (5ft)								
						10m (33ft)	12m (40ft)		
						10m (33ft)	12m (40ft)		
								6m (20ft)	9m (30ft)
		1m (3ft)	1m (3ft)						
3.5m (11ft)	2.25m (7ft)								

	Columnar		Conical	
	Height	Spread	Height	Spread
Cercis siliquastrum, 93, 151			9m (30ft)	4.5m (15ft)
Chaenomeles speciosa, 15				
Chamaecyparis lawsoniana Allumii, 181, 182	12m (40ft)	4.5m (15ft)		
Columnaris, 139, 181	7m (23ft)	1m (3ft)		
Ellwoodii, 181	3m (10ft)	75cm (30in)		
Erecta, 181	15m (50ft)	4.5m (15ft)		
Fletcheri, 143, 181	6m (20ft)	2m (6ft)		
Fraseri, 183	12m (40ft)	4.5m (15ft)		
Headfort, 183			5m (16ft)	4m (13ft)
Kilmacurragh, 62, 183	15m (50ft)	2.25m (7ft)		
Pembury Blue, 131, 183			10m (33ft)	4m (13ft)
Pottenii, 39, 42, 183	12m (40ft)	3.5m (11ft)		
Winston Churchill, 48, 183	6m (20ft)	2m (6ft)		
nootkatensis Pendula, 183, 184				
obtusa, 185			12m (40ft)	10m (33ft)
Crippsii, 185			7.5m (25ft)	5m (16ft)
Nana Gracilis, 185			3m (10ft)	2m (6ft)
pisifera, 185			6m (20ft)	4.5m (15ft)
Chionanthus virginicus, 143				
Clethra barbinervis, 60				

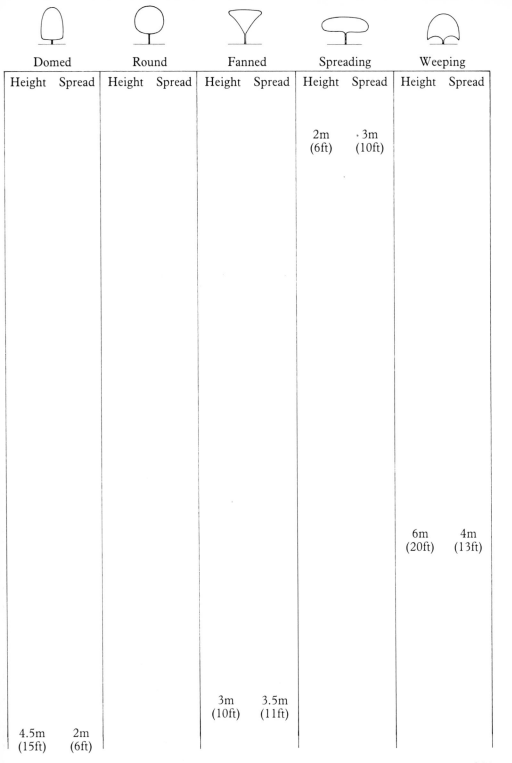

Domed		Round		Fanned		Spreading		Weeping	
Height	Spread	Height	Spread	Height	Spread	Height	Spread	Height	Spread
						2m (6ft)	·3m (10ft)		
								6m (20ft)	4m (13ft)
				3m (10ft)	3.5m (11ft)				
4.5m (15ft)	2m (6ft)								

	Columnar		Conical	
	Height	Spread	Height	Spread
Cornus alba vars., 11, 15				
controversa, 143				
florida, 174				
Cherokee Chief, 176				
kousa, 111				
mas, 162, 163				
nuttallii, 88			7m (23ft)	4.5m (15ft)
Corylopsis veitchiana, 156, 157				
Corylus avellana Aurea, 15				
maxima Purpurea, 15				
Cotinus coggygria Royal Purple, 93, 95, 110				
Crataegus chlorosarca, 124				
coccinioides, 85				
crus-galli Pyracanthifolia, 144				
ellwangerana, 155				
intricata, 124				
laevigata Paul's Scarlet, 126, 130				
Rosea Flore Pleno, 58				
× lavallei, 131				
maximowiczii, 83				

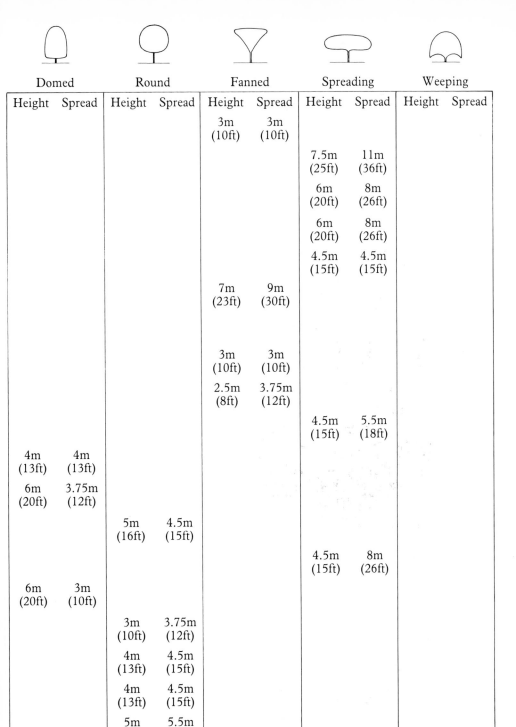

Domed		Round		Fanned		Spreading		Weeping	
Height	Spread	Height	Spread	Height	Spread	Height	Spread	Height	Spread
				3m (10ft)	3m (10ft)				
						7.5m (25ft)	11m (36ft)		
						6m (20ft)	8m (26ft)		
						6m (20ft)	8m (26ft)		
						4.5m (15ft)	4.5m (15ft)		
				7m (23ft)	9m (30ft)				
				3m (10ft)	3m (10ft)				
				2.5m (8ft)	3.75m (12ft)				
						4.5m (15ft)	5.5m (18ft)		
4m (13ft)	4m (13ft)								
6m (20ft)	3.75m (12ft)								
		5m (16ft)	4.5m (15ft)						
						4.5m (15ft)	8m (26ft)		
6m (20ft)	3m (10ft)								
		3m (10ft)	3.75m (12ft)						
		4m (13ft)	4.5m (15ft)						
		4m (13ft)	4.5m (15ft)						
		5m (16ft)	5.5m (18ft)						
5m (16ft)	4m (13ft)								

	Columnar		Conical	
	Height	Spread	Height	Spread
Crataegus mollis, 173				
monogyna Stricta, 85				
rivularis, 124				
tomentosa, 155				
Cryptomeria japonica, 185			20m (65ft)	10m (33ft)
× *Cupressocyparis leylandii,* 185			25m (80ft)	18m (60ft)
Cupressus glabra Pyramidalis, 43, 185	15m (50ft)	5m (16ft)		
macrocarpa Donard Gold, 186			15m (50ft)	6m (20ft)
Goldcrest, 186			15m (50ft)	4.5m (15ft)
sempervirens Stricta, 186	25m (80ft)	5.5m (18ft)		
Davidia involucrata, 136				
Diospyros lotus, 66			4.5m (15ft)	2.5m (8ft)
virginiana, 83			5.5m (18ft)	2.75m (9ft)
Elaeagnus × *ebbingei,* 144, 153				
pungens Maculata, 14, 139, 153				
Embothrium coccineum lanceolatum, 133, 147	10m (33ft)	2.75m (9ft)		
Eucryphia glutinosa, 29, 32	4m (13ft)	1m (3ft)		
× *intermedia* Rostrevor, 111	6m (20ft)	3.5m (11ft)		
× *nymansensis* Nymansay, 34	5m (16ft)	2m (6ft)		

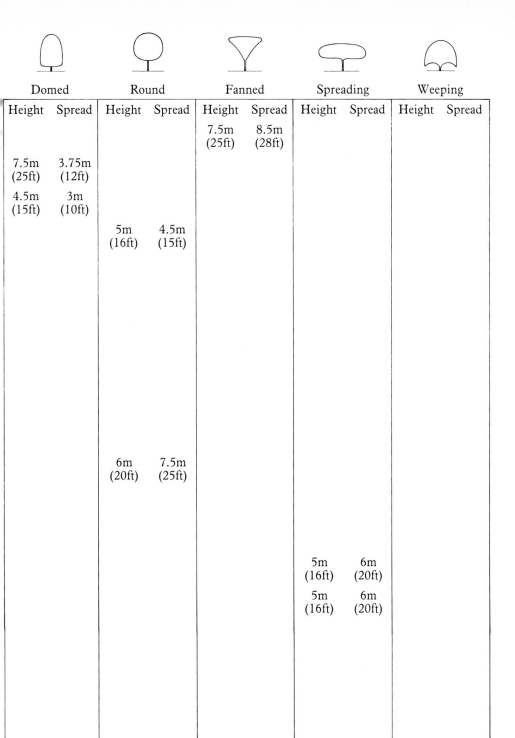

	Domed		Round		Fanned		Spreading		Weeping
	Height	Spread	Height	Spread	Height	Spread	Height	Spread	Height	Spread
					7.5m (25ft)	8.5m (28ft)				
	7.5m (25ft)	3.75m (12ft)								
	4.5m (15ft)	3m (10ft)								
			5m (16ft)	4.5m (15ft)						
			6m (20ft)	7.5m (25ft)						
							5m (16ft)	6m (20ft)		
							5m (16ft)	6m (20ft)		

207

	Columnar		Conical	
	Height	Spread	Height	Spread
Euonymus japonicus, 16				
semiexsertus, 85				
Fagus sylvatica Dawyck, 191			20m (65ft)	5m (16ft)
Purple Dawyck, 143, 191	10m (33ft)	3m (10ft)		
Purpurea Pendula, 192, 193				
Fontanesia phillyreoides, 73				
Forsythia × *intermedia* Lynwood, 16				
Frangula alnus, 126				
Fraxinus excelsior Pendula, 193				
Ginkgo biloba, 193			30m (100ft)	10m (33ft)
Fastigiata, 193	30m (100ft)	6m (20ft)		
Pendula, 85				
Gleditsia triacanthos Sunburst, 151, 167				
Halesia carolina, 88				
monticola vestita, 102				
Hamamelis mollis, 51				
Hibiscus syriacus, 85				
Hypericum androsaemum, 16, 37				
Hidcote, 16, 137, 138				

Domed		Round		Fanned		Spreading		Weeping	
Height	Spread	Height	Spread	Height	Spread	Height	Spread	Height	Spread
		3.75m (12ft)	3.75m (12ft)						
		3m (10ft)	3m (10ft)						
								8m (26ft)	8m (26ft)
		4.5m (15ft)	4m (13ft)						
				2m (6ft)	3m (10ft)				
				4.5m (15ft)	4.5m (15ft)				
								20m (65ft)	15m (50ft)
								4.5m (15ft)	6m (20ft)
				7.5m (25ft)	9m (30ft)				
4m (13ft)	4m (13ft)								
9m (30ft)	6m (20ft)								
				4m (13ft)	5m (16ft)				
4m (13ft)	2.5m (8ft)								
75cm (30in)	50cm (20in)								
1.5m (5ft)	2m (6ft)								

	Columnar		Conical	
	Height	Spread	Height	Spread
Ilex aquifolium vars., 193				
Juniperus chinensis, 28, 30, 186	6m (20ft)	2.5m (8ft)		
Fairview, 186	3m (10ft)	75cm (30in)		
Iowa, 187	6m (20ft)	1.25m (4ft)		
communis Hibernica, 187	4m (13ft)	50cm (18in)		
virginiana Skyrocket, 58, 60, 187	4m (13ft)	25cm (10in)		
Kerria japonica, 17, 18				
Laburnum alpinum, 144, 146				
Pendulum, 51				
anagyroides Erect, 60	7.5m (25ft)	1.5m (5ft)		
× *watereri* Vossii, 190				
Liquidambar styraciflua, 190			20m (65ft)	8m (26ft)
Maackia chinensis, 73, 75				
Magnolia Charles Coates, 119, 120				
cordata, 34				
dawsoniana, 34			3m (10ft)	1.75m (5ft)
denudata, 122				
Kewensis, 119			6m (20ft)	3.5m (11ft)
× *loebneri*, 122				

Domed		Round		Fanned		Spreading		Weeping	
Height	Spread	Height	Spread	Height	Spread	Height	Spread	Height	Spread
		6m (20ft)	4.5m (15ft)						
				2m (6ft)	2m (6ft)				
		5.5m (18ft)	5m (16ft)						
								2m (6ft)	2.5m (8ft)
				6m (20ft)	6m (20ft)				
5m (16ft)	5m (16ft)								
6m (20ft)	5m (16ft)								
		3m (10ft)	3.5m (11ft)						
6m (20ft)	6m (20ft)								
4.5m (15ft)	3m (10ft)								

211

	Columnar		Conical	
	Height	Spread	Height	Spread
Magnolia × *loebneri*				
Leonard Messel, 62			5m (16ft)	3.25m (11ft)
salicifolia, 122				
sargentiana, 119			10m (33ft)	5m (16ft)
robusta, 122				
× *soulangiana* Lennei, 163				
Rustica Rubra, 163				
stellata, 119				
Rosea, 119				
Rubra, 122				
× *veitchii*, 171				
Malus Almey, 66				
× *atrosanguinea*, 156				
Chilko, 173				
Echtermeyer, 136				
Elise Rathke, 83				
Exzellenz Thiel, 46				
florentina, 96				
floribunda, 106				
glaucescens, 88				

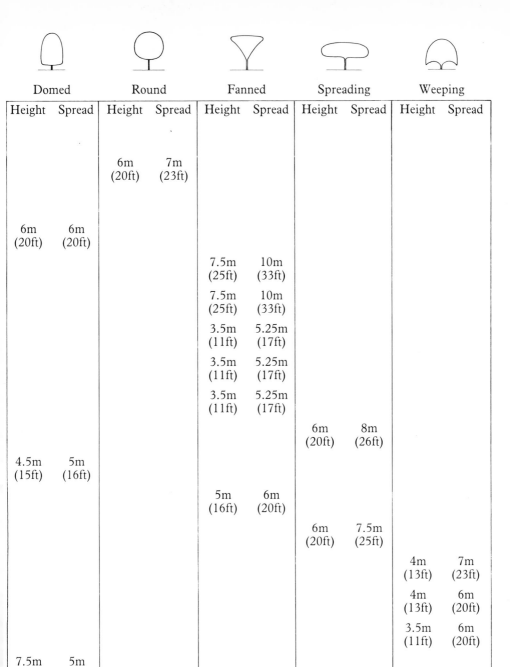

Domed		Round		Fanned		Spreading		Weeping	
Height	Spread	Height	Spread	Height	Spread	Height	Spread	Height	Spread
		6m (20ft)	7m (23ft)						
6m (20ft)	6m (20ft)								
				7.5m (25ft)	10m (33ft)				
				7.5m (25ft)	10m (33ft)				
				3.5m (11ft)	5.25m (17ft)				
				3.5m (11ft)	5.25m (17ft)				
				3.5m (11ft)	5.25m (17ft)				
						6m (20ft)	8m (26ft)		
4.5m (15ft)	5m (16ft)								
				5m (16ft)	6m (20ft)				
						6m (20ft)	7.5m (25ft)		
								4m (13ft)	7m (23ft)
								4m (13ft)	6m (20ft)
								3.5m (11ft)	6m (20ft)
7.5m (25ft)	5m (16ft)								
								8m (26ft)	10m (33ft)
		5m (16ft)	4.5m (15ft)						

	Columnar		Conical	
	Height	Spread	Height	Spread
Malus halliana Parkmanii, 155				
hupehensis, 166				
Kaido, 88				
Katherine, 139, 141				
Lady Northcliffe, 46				
prunifolia, 166				
Fastigiata, 96				
Red Jade, 66				
sieboldii, 47				
sikkimensis, 101				
spectabilis, 96				
× sublobata, 28			6m (20ft)	3.5m (11ft)
toringoides, 135				
trilobata, 45	7.5m (26ft)	3.5m (11ft)		
Van Eseltine, 62	5m (16ft)	1m (3ft)		
Wintergold, 91				
yunnanensis veitchii, 46			6m (20ft)	3.75m (12ft)
× zumi, 35	3.5m (11ft)	1.75m (6ft)		
Morus alba Pendula, 62				

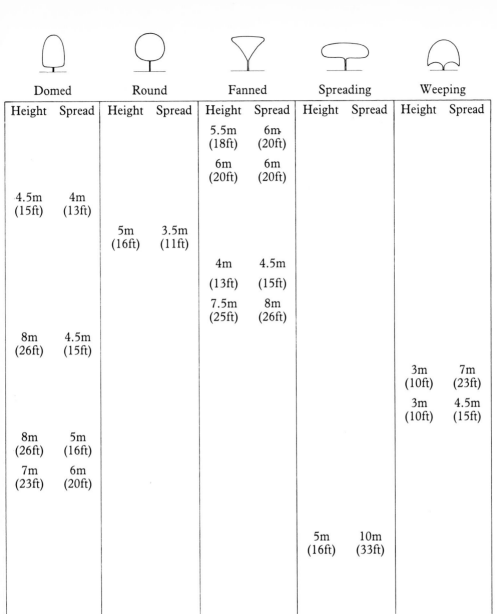

	Domed		Round		Fanned		Spreading		Weeping	
	Height	Spread	Height	Spread	Height	Spread	Height	Spread	Height	Spread
					5.5m (18ft)	6m (20ft)				
					6m (20ft)	6m (20ft)				
	4.5m (15ft)	4m (13ft)								
			5m (16ft)	3.5m (11ft)						
					4m (13ft)	4.5m (15ft)				
					7.5m (25ft)	8m (26ft)				
	8m (26ft)	4.5m (15ft)								
									3m (10ft)	7m (23ft)
									3m (10ft)	4.5m (15ft)
	8m (26ft)	5m (16ft)								
	7m (23ft)	6m (20ft)								
							5m (16ft)	10m (33ft)		
			4m (13ft)	3.5m (12ft)						
									3m (10ft)	3m (10ft)

	Columnar		Conical	
	Height	Spread	Height	Spread
Morus alba Pyramidalis, 69	5m (16ft)	1m (3ft)		
Ostrya japonica, 136			8m (26ft)	6m (20ft)
Oxydendrum arboreum, 111			7m (23ft)	3.5m (11ft)
Parrotiopsis jacquemontiana, 147			6m (20ft)	4m (13ft)
Paulownia tomentosa, 99, 176				
Philadelphus Virginal, 18, 19				
Picea abies Pyramidata, 187	20m (65ft)	4m (13ft)		
breweriana, 187				
omorika, 188	18m (60ft)	3.75m (12ft)		
pungens glauca, 188			25m (80ft)	10m (33ft)
smithiana, 188				
Pinus cembra, 53, 188			6m (20ft)	3m (10ft)
peuce, 188			10m (33ft)	5m (16ft)
Potentilla fruticosa Elizabeth, 18, 57				
Katherine Dykes, 18				
Prunus Accolade, 100, 106				
Amanogawa, 10, 58	8m (26ft)	1m (3ft)		
× *amygdalo-persica* Pollardii, 131				
Asano, 39				

216

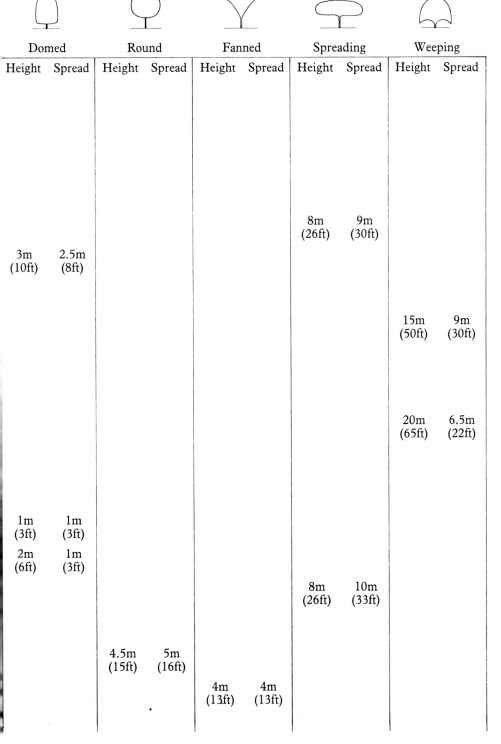

Domed		Round		Fanned		Spreading		Weeping	
Height	Spread	Height	Spread	Height	Spread	Height	Spread	Height	Spread
						8m (26ft)	9m (30ft)		
3m (10ft)	2.5m (8ft)								
								15m (50ft)	9m (30ft)
								20m (65ft)	6.5m (22ft)
1m (3ft)	1m (3ft)								
2m (6ft)	1m (3ft)								
						8m (26ft)	10m (33ft)		
		4.5m (15ft)	5m (16ft)						
				4m (13ft)	4m (13ft)				

	Columnar		Conical	
	Height	Spread	Height	Spread

Prunus avium Pendula, 43

  Botan Zakura, 160

  cerasifera Nigra, 48

    Pendula, 135

    Pissardii, 68

  cerasus Semperflorens, 91

  Cheal's Weeping Cherry, 25, 59

  × *hillieri*, 162

    Spire, 68   7.5m (25ft)   3m (10ft)

  Hilling's Weeping Cherry, 28

  Hisakura, 43

  Horinji, 150

  Ichiyo, 171

  incisa, 168

    Moerheimii, 39

  Ito-kukuri, 45

  Kanzan, 100, 162

  Kiku-shidare Sakura, 27, 58, 60

  kurilensis Ruby, 68   5m (16ft)   1.5m (5ft)

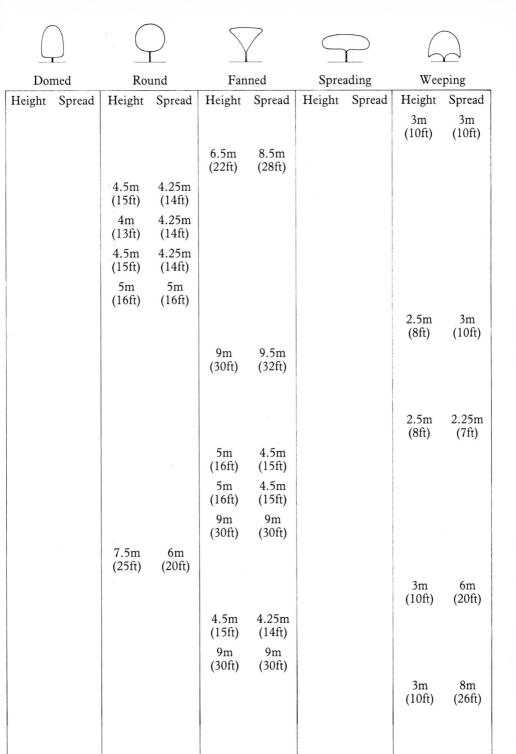

Domed		Round		Fanned		Spreading		Weeping	
Height	Spread	Height	Spread	Height	Spread	Height	Spread	Height	Spread
								3m (10ft)	3m (10ft)
				6.5m (22ft)	8.5m (28ft)				
		4.5m (15ft)	4.25m (14ft)						
		4m (13ft)	4.25m (14ft)						
		4.5m (15ft)	4.25m (14ft)						
		5m (16ft)	5m (16ft)						
								2.5m (8ft)	3m (10ft)
				9m (30ft)	9.5m (32ft)				
								2.5m (8ft)	2.25m (7ft)
				5m (16ft)	4.5m (15ft)				
				5m (16ft)	4.5m (15ft)				
				9m (30ft)	9m (30ft)				
		7.5m (25ft)	6m (20ft)						
								3m (10ft)	6m (20ft)
				4.5m (15ft)	4.25m (14ft)				
				9m (30ft)	9m (30ft)				
								3m (10ft)	8m (26ft)

	Columnar		Conical	
	Height	Spread	Height	Spread
Prunus Kursar, 156				
lusitanica, 18, 95				
Mikuruma-gaeshi, 160				
Pink Perfection, 160				
Pink Shell, 68				
pseudocerasus Cantabrigiensis, 150				
serrula, 155				
serrulata, 168				
Shimidsu Sakura, 126				
Shirotae, 77, 80				
Shosar, 77, 79			7.5m (25ft)	4.5m (15ft)
simonii, 131				
Snow Goose, 150				
subhirtella Stellata, 150				
Taizanfukun, 25			6.5m (22ft)	3.5m (11ft)
Taoyama Zakura, 88				
Ukon, 168				
Umineko, 25	4m (13ft)	2.25m (7ft)		
× *yedoensis* Shidare Yoshino, 60				

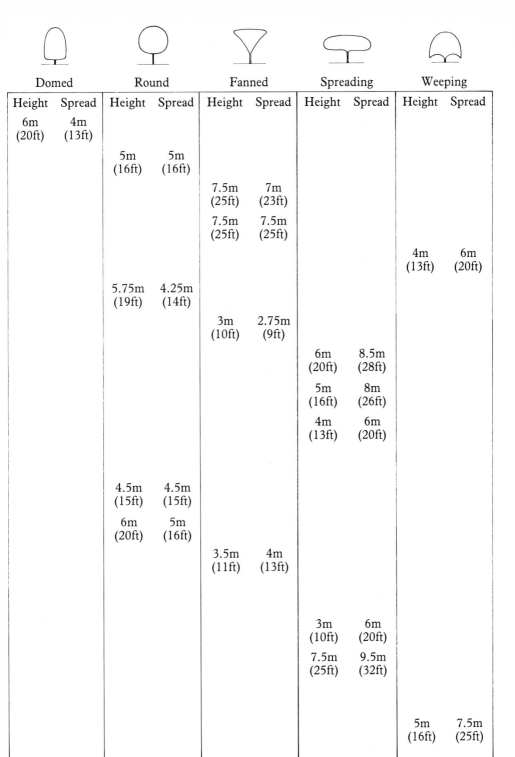

Domed		Round		Fanned		Spreading		Weeping	
Height	Spread	Height	Spread	Height	Spread	Height	Spread	Height	Spread
6m (20ft)	4m (13ft)								
		5m (16ft)	5m (16ft)						
				7.5m (25ft)	7m (23ft)				
				7.5m (25ft)	7.5m (25ft)				
								4m (13ft)	6m (20ft)
		5.75m (19ft)	4.25m (14ft)						
				3m (10ft)	2.75m (9ft)				
						6m (20ft)	8.5m (28ft)		
						5m (16ft)	8m (26ft)		
						4m (13ft)	6m (20ft)		
		4.5m (15ft)	4.5m (15ft)						
		6m (20ft)	5m (16ft)						
				3.5m (11ft)	4m (13ft)				
						3m (10ft)	6m (20ft)		
						7.5m (25ft)	9.5m (32ft)		
								5m (16ft)	7.5m (25ft)

221

	Columnar		Conical	
	Height	Spread	Height	Spread
Prunus Yokihi, 47				
Pyrus salicifolia Pendula, 91				
Rhus typhina, 93, 96				
Ribes sanguineum, 10, 18				
Robinia pseudoacacia Bessoniana, 143				
Frisia, 93, 95, 191				
Pyramidalis, 51	9m (30ft)	2m (6ft)		
Rosmarinus officinalis Miss Jessop's Variety, 18				
Severn Sea, 19				
Salix alba Chermesina, 11, 48, 50, 105				
Sericea, 103				
Vitellina, 49, 105, 156				
caprea Kilmarnock, 29				
× *chrysocoma*, 126, 194				
Sambucus nigra Aurea, 19, 20				
Skimmia japonica, 19				
Sorbaronia × *sorbifolia*, 124				
Sorbus americana, 144	9m (30ft)	3.5m (11ft)		
aucuparia Sheerwater Seedling, 37			6m (20ft)	4.5m (15ft)

Domed		Round		Fanned		Spreading		Weeping	
Height	Spread	Height	Spread	Height	Spread	Height	Spread	Height	Spread
				4m (13ft)	4m (13ft)				
								3.5m (11ft)	3.5m (11ft)
		3m (10ft)	3m (10ft)						
2m (6ft)	2m (6ft)								
		6m (20ft)	3.75m (12ft)						
6m (20ft)	4.5m (15ft)								
2m (6ft)	1m (3ft)								
				50cm (20in)	1m (3ft)				
7m (23ft)	8m (26ft)			4m (13ft)	4m (13ft)*				
7m (23ft)	8m (26ft)								
7m (23ft)	8m (26ft)			4m (13ft)	4m (13ft)*				
								3m (10ft)	2.25m (7ft)
								18m (60ft)	18m (60ft)
		4m (13ft)	4m (13ft)						
1m (3ft)	1m (3ft)								
				2.5m (8ft)	3m (10ft)				

*If cut hard back every second spring

223

	Columnar		Conical	
	Height	Spread	Height	Spread
Sorbus bristoliensis, 101				
cashmiriana, 37				
chamaemespilus, 37				
commixta, 114			7m (23ft)	4m (13ft)
Embley, 35	6m (20ft)	2.25m (7ft)		
Ethel's Gold, 83	7.5m (25ft)	2.75m (9ft)		
folgneri Lemon Drop, 173				
graeca, 114				
hupehensis, 166				
insignis, 101				
Jermyns, 47			8m (26ft)	4m (13ft)
meinichii, 124, 134			7m (23ft)	4m (13ft)
meliosmifolia, 144	7.5m (25ft)	3m (10ft)		
mougeotii, 114				
pohuashanensis, 114			10m (33ft)	6m (20ft)
poteriifolia, 114				
Signalman, 66	6m (20ft)	2.5m (8ft)		
× *thuringiaca,* 103				
Fastigiata, 114, 115			6m (20ft)	4m (13ft)

Domed		Round		Fanned		Spreading		Weeping	
Height	Spread	Height	Spread	Height	Spread	Height	Spread	Height	Spread
7.5m (25ft)	6m (20ft)								
4m (13ft)	3.5m (11ft)								
		3m (10ft)	2.5m (8ft)						
						6m (20ft)	8m (26ft)		
4.5m (15ft)	4m (13ft)								
				7m (23ft)	5.5m (18ft)				
7m (23ft)	4.5m (15ft)								
4.5m (15ft)	3m (10ft)								
6m (20ft)	3.5m (11ft)								
9m (30ft)	6m (20ft)								

225

	Columnar		Conical	
	Height	Spread	Height	Spread
Sorbus vilmorinii, 77				
Staphylea holocarpa Rosea, 147, 149				
pinnata, 111				
Stewartia koreana, 29	5m (16ft)	2.25m (7ft)		
monodelpha, 73			5m (16ft)	3m (10ft)
pseudocamellia, 73	8m (26ft)	2m (6ft)		
Styrax obassia, 126			8.5m (28ft)	4.5m (15ft)
serrulata, 111				
Syringa vulgaris vars., 60, 77				
Tamarix pentandra, 93				
Taxus baccata Elegantissima, 189			6m (20ft)	6m (20ft)
Fastigiata, 53, 189	5.5m (18ft)	2.25m (7ft)		
Fastigiata Aurea, 69, 72, 189	4.5m (15ft)	2m (6ft)		
Thuja plicata Zebrina, 189			25m (80ft)	12m (40ft)
Viburnum plicatum tomentosum, 21				
Mariesii, 21, 22				
Weigela spp. and vars., 21				
Xanthoceras sorbifolium, 163, 165				

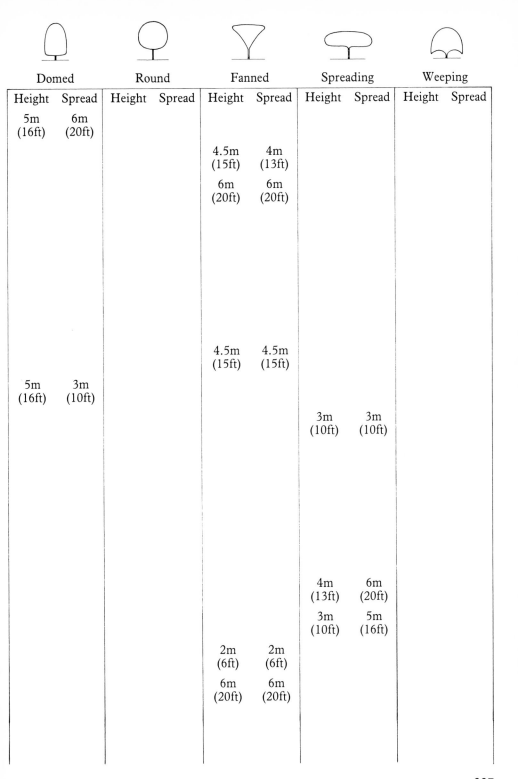

Domed		Round		Fanned		Spreading		Weeping	
Height	Spread	Height	Spread	Height	Spread	Height	Spread	Height	Spread
5m (16ft)	6m (20ft)								
				4.5m (15ft)	4m (13ft)				
				6m (20ft)	6m (20ft)				
				4.5m (15ft)	4.5m (15ft)				
5m (16ft)	3m (10ft)								
						3m (10ft)	3m (10ft)		
						4m (13ft)	6m (20ft)		
						3m (10ft)	5m (16ft)		
				2m (6ft)	2m (6ft)				
				6m (20ft)	6m (20ft)				

Index

acacia, false, 51, **52**, 94, **95**, 143–4, 191
Acer, 53, **55**, 63, **65**, 69, 84, 103, 106, 107, **109**, 139, 147, **148**, **152**, 167, 174
aconite, 28
Aesculus, 35–7, 91, **92**, 102, **103**, 189
Ajuga reptans, 31
alder buckthorn, 130
almond, hybrid, 135
Amelanchier, 111, 139, 174, **175**
Anemone blanda, 43
apricot plum, 135
Arbrex, 11
Arbutus unedo, 189
Arctostaphylos uva-ursi, 76
Armillatox, 12
ash, flowering, 145, 190
manna, 190
weeping, 193
aster, 69
astilbe, 150
aucuba, 15
autumn tints, 31, 37, 41, 44, 46, 47, 48, 52, 55, 57, 61, 65, 69, 71, 73, 77, 83, 84, 87, 89, 90, 91, 95, 98, 102, 106, 109, 110, 111, 113, 116, 125, 126, 136, 139, 143, 145, 148, 155, 162, 166, 167, 170, 175, 190

barberry, 69 *see also Berberis*
bark, ornamental, 11, 15, 31, 44, 49, 57, 68, 75, 76, 83, 85, 94, 105, 106, 107, 109, 110, 129, 131, 148, 155, 156, 167, 191
bear grape, 76
beech, Dawyck, 143, 191
Purple Dawyck, 143, 191
weeping purple, **192**, 193
Berberis, 15, 69
bergenia, 29
Betula, 131, **132**, 190
birch, weeping silver, 131, **132**, 190
bladdernut, 111, 114
bluebell, 43, 107, 114, 177
Bray's Emulsion, 12

broadleaf trees, formal, 179
informal, 189–91
semi-formal, 191–4
bronzeleaf, 39
buckeye, Californian, 102
Ohio, 102, **103**
red, 91
small, 35–7
see also Aesculus
buddleia, 11, 15, **16**, **45**
bugle, 31
bulbs, 28, 32, 43, 71, 107, 114, 122, 177

camellia, 15
Catalpa, 171, **172**, 176
catmint, 63
cedar, Atlas, 179
blue, 179, **180**
deodar, 179
incense, 181
Japanese, 185
of Lebanon, 180
western red, 189
Cedrus, 179, **180**
Ceratostigma willmottianum, 15
Cercis, 93, **94**, **151**
Chaenomeles speciosa, 15
Chamaecyparis, 39, **42**, 48, 62, 131, 139, 143, 181, **182**, 183, **184**, 185
cherry, All Saints, 91
Cambridge, 150, 153
Cornelian, 162, **163**
Fuji, 41, 69, 153, 162, 170
Japanese alpine, 69
Lombardy poplar, 10
Oshima, 153
spring, 106, 150, 153
wild weeping, 43–4
Yoshino, 61
see also Prunus
chionodoxa, 28, 107, 122
chokeberry, 126
Christmas box, 51
chrysanthemum, 135
cinquefoil, 18 *see also* potentilla
Clematis montana, 144
viticella, 167
clipping, 10–11
cockspur thorn, 135, 145

conifers, 10, 28, 30, 39, **42**, 43, 48, 53, **56**, 58, 60, 62, 69, 71, **72**, 131, 139, 143, 179, **180**, 181, **182**, 183, **184**, 185–9
formal, 179
informal, 179–80
semi-formal, 181–9
Convallaria majalis, 166 *see also* lily of the valley
coppicing, 11, 49, 124, 158
Cornus alba, 11, 15
kousa, 111, **112**
mas, 162, **163**
Corylopsis, 156, **157**
Cotinus, 93, **95**, 110
crabapple, *see Malus* in Summary
Crataegus, **58**, 83, 85, **88**, 124, 126, **130**, 131, 144, 155, **173**
crocus, 28, 107
currant, flowering, 18 *see also Ribes*
cypress, Arizona, 44, 185
Gowen, 186
Hinoki, 185
Italian, 186
Lawson's, 181–3
Leyland, 185
Mediterranean, 186
Monterey, 186
Nootka, 183, 184
Sawara, 185
smooth, 44, 185
see also Chamaecyparis, × Cupressocyparis and *Cupressus* in Summary

daffodil, 107
dahlia, 46, 62, 135
damage to foundations, 49, 105, 158
date plum, 67
Davidia, 136, **137**
diseases, tree, 11–12
dogwood, flowering, **81**, 175–6, 177
Japanese, 143 *see also Cornus kousa*
red-barked, 15 *see also Cornus alba*
western, 88, 89–90

Elaeagnus, 14, 141, **142**, 145, 153
elder, golden, 19, **20**
Embothrium, **133**, 147, 150
Enmag, 9, 12
Eranthis hyemalis, 28
Erica, 106 *see also* heather
eucalyptus, 191
eucryphia, 29 – 30, **32**, 34, 113
Euonymus fortunei radicans, 90
exhaust fumes, 52, 124, 163, 173

Fagus, 143, 191, **192**
feathered stems, 10, 71, 88
ferns, 71, 131
fertiliser, 9 – 10, 12
filbert, 15
firebush, Norquinco Valley, **133**, 147, 150
foam flower, 44
foliar feed, 12
Fontanesia, 73, 76, **77**
forsythia, 16
foundations, damage to, 49, 105, 158
foxglove, 162
tree, **99**, 177
fringe tree, 144
frost, 119
fungal infection, 11 – 12

Galax urceolata, 166
garlic, wild, 130 – 1
geranium, 142 – 3
Ginkgo, 85, **193**
Gleditsia, **151**, 167
gorse, Spanish, 16
grading of trees, 10
grape hyacinth, 43, 107, 122
Growmore, 12
gum tree, 190, 191

Halesia, 88, **90**
half-standard trees, 10
handkerchief tree, 136, **137**
hawthorn, American, 87, 124 – 5, 135, 155, 174
double pink, **58**
double scarlet, 129, **130**
red, **173**, 174
Siberian, 83
umbrella, 145, 147
upright, 87, **88**
see also Crataegus
hazel, 15
heather, 45, 105 – 6
Hebe, 16, 117

Hedera helix, 93
holly, 14, 193 – 4
honey fungus, 11
locust, **151**, 167 – 8
hop hornbeam, 137
hornbeam, 179
horse chestnut, 189
Hosta, 124, 131, 176
hydrangea, blue, 114
climbing, 98
hypericum, 11, 16, 37, 137, **138**

Indian bean tree, 171, **172**, 176
industrial pollution, 52, 124, 135, 144, 155, 163, 168, 173
iris, 131
island bed, 126, 135
ivy, variegated, 93

jasmine, white climbing, 156
winter-flowering, 88
Judas tree, 93, **94**, **151**
juneberry, 111, 139
Chinese, **175**
juniper, Chinese, 28, 29, **30**, 186 – 7
creeping, 43
Irish, 187
Skyrocket, 58 – 9, **60**, 187
Juniperus, 28 – 9, **30**, 43, 58 – 9, **60**, 186 – 7

Kerria, **17**, 18
knotgrass, creeping, 47

laburnum, common upright, 60, **61**
hybrid, 190
Scotch, 144, **146**, 147
Scotch weeping, 51, 53
laurel, common, 18, 131
Portugal, 18, 95
Lavatera, 176
lavender, 48, 63
leaf mould, 12
lilac, 60, 78, 80
lily, 176
of the valley, 131, 166
plantain, *see Hosta*
lime, weeping silver, 191
Liriodendron, **190**, 191
London pride, 102
Luzula maxima, 172

Maackia, 73, **75**
magnolia, 34, **35**, 62 – 3, 119, **120**, **121**, 122 – 4, 163, **164**, 171

Mahonia, 62
Maianthemum bifolium, 166
maidenhair tree, **193**
upright, 193
weeping, 87
mallow, shrubby, 85, 87
Malus, 28, 35, 45, 46, 47, 62, 66, 83, 88, 91, 96, 101, 106, 135, 136, 139, **141**, 155, 156, 166, 173
manure, 119
maple, bigleaf, 84
bigtooth, 84
Canadian, 53, 55, 107
Chinese, 85, 167
coral-bark, 147, **148**, **152**
Father David's, 106, 107 – 10
hawthorn-leaved, 107, 110
Henry's, 167
Japanese, 53, **55**, 57, 63, 66, 69, 71, 91, 107, 110, 147 – 8, 152, 167
fig-leaf, 91
purple cut-leaved, 69, 71
yellow, 107, **109**, 110
yellow cut-leaved, 57
Montpelier, 84, 176
Norway, **65**
purple, 191
Oregon, 84
red, 53, 55, 66, 107, 110
rock, 103
sugar, 65
swamp, 55, 107
see also Acer
marigold, 135
may, double pink, **58**
double scarlet, 126, **130**
see also Crataegus
Michaelmas daisy, 84
mock orange, 18, **19**
monkey puzzle, 179
Morus, 62, 69, **70**
mountain ash, *see Sorbus* in Summary
mulberry, white, upright, **70**, 71
weeping, 62
see also Morus
mulch, 12
myrobalan, 48 – 9, **68**, 135
weeping, 136

nutrient deficiency, 12

Oxydendrum, 111, **113**

paint, bituminous, 11

Parrotia persica, 149
partridge berry, 66, 102
Paulownia, **99**, 176
pear, willow-leaved, 91, 93
peat, 9, 73, 113–4, 119, 129, 163
peony, 131, 150, 176
periwinkle, 168
persimmon, 67, 83–4
petunia, 176
Philadelphus, 18, **19**
pine, Arolla, 57, 188
　Austrian, 180
　Bhutan, 188
　Chile, 179
　Corsican, 180
　Macedonian, 188
　Scots, 180–1
plantain lily, 124, 131, 176
planting, 9–10
plum, purple-leaved, 49, 68
pollarding, 49, 158
Polygonum affine, 47
　campanulatum, 34
potassium, 12, 34
potentilla, 18, 57
primrose, 62
pruning, 10–11, 25, 28, 46, 47, 49, 75, 91, 98, 105, 109, 116, 124, 128, 160, 162
Prunus, 10, 18, 25, 28, 39, **41**, 43, 45, 47, 48, 58, **60**, **68**, 77, **79**, **80**, 88, 91, **100**, 106, 126, 131, 135, 150, 155, **156**, 160, **161**, 162, 168, 171

quickthorn, 87

rhododendron, 18, 131, 161
　winter-flowering, 53
Rhus, 93, **96**
Ribes, 10–11, 18
Robinia, 51, **52**, 93, **95**, 143, 191
Rodgersia aesculifolia, 39
rose, shrub, 126, 158, 174
　weeping standard, 194–5
rosemary, 18–19
rose of Sharon, American, 85
　English, 18, 80
rowan, *see Sorbus* in Summary

Salix, 11, 29, **31**, 48, **50**, 103, 105, 126, **128**, 156, 194
Santolina chamaecyparissus, 59
Sarcococca confusa, 51
saxifrage, 102
screen, 53, 88, 147, 160

Senecio greyi, 19, **21**, 59
Sidalcea, 69
site, average, 35, 37, 51, 93, 103, 124, 144, 155, 156, 160, 162, 166, 168
　sheltered, 29, 43, 53, 62, 65, 71, 73, 84, 89, 107, 111, 119, 122, 136, 147, 167, 171, 176
　sunny, 25, 28, 41, 43, 45, 47, 48, 51, 58, 60, 66, 68, 77, 83, 85, 91, 98, 101, 102, 106, 114, 131, 139, 143, 147, 150, 156, 160, 166, 168, 173, 175
　woodland, 34, 73, 107, 111, 119, 122, 128, 147, 163, 167, 176
Skimmia, 19
smoke tree, purple-leaved, 94, **95**, 110
snowball bush, 21
snowbell, Himalayan, 111
　Japanese, 129
snowdrop, 107
　tree, 89, **90**
　　mountain, 102
soil, clay, 91, 114, 119, 122, 144, 155, 163
　dry, 43, 68, 77, 85, 114, 124, 144, 167, 173
　lime-free, 29, 34, 53, 71, 73, 89, 102, 111, 119, 122, 147, 163, 171, 175
　moist, 60, 62, 73, 111, 119, 122, 128, 147, 171, 175
　normal, 25, 28, 35, 37, 41, 43, 45, 47, 51, 58, 65, 66, 68, 77, 83, 84, 85, 91, 93, 98, 101, 103, 106, 107, 114, 131, 136, 139, 143, 150, 155, 156, 160, 162, 166, 167, 168, 173, 175, 176
　sandy, 51, 68, 77, 91, 114, 144, 155, 163
Sorbaronia, 126
Sorbus, 35, **36**, 37, **38**, 47, 66, 77, **78**, 83, 101, 103, **104**, 114, **115**, **117**, 124, **125**, **134**, 144, 173
sorrel tree, 111, **113**
Spanish gorse, 16
spindle tree, Japanese, 16, 87
spruce, blue, 188
　Brewer's, 187
　Colorado, 188
　Norway, 187
　Serbian, 188
　Smith's, 188
　weeping, 187, 188

Stachys lanata, 59
staking, 10
Staphylea, 111, 147, **149**
stem-rot, 11
stewartia, 29–30, 73–5, **76**
strawberry tree, 189
sumach, stag's horn, 95, **96**
sweet gum, 190
sycamore, 84, 189

tamarisk, 95
Taxus, 53, **56**, 69, **72**, 189
thyme, golden lemon-scented, 45
trace elements, 12
tree of heaven, 189
tulip tree, **190**, 191
　pink, 171
tutsan, 16, 37

veronica, shrubby, 16, 117
Viburnum, 19, 21, **22**, 67
vine, giant, 170
violet, 53

wake robin, 176
wallflower, 135
watering, 9, 12
Weeping Sally, 31
Weigela, 21
whitebeam, *see Sorbus* in Summary
willow, goat, 29, **31**
　golden weeping, **128**, 194
　Kilmarnock, 29, **31**
　red-barked, 11, 48, **50**, 105
　silver-leaved, 103
　white, 11, 48, 103, 105, 156
　yellow-barked, 11, 105, 156
　see also Salix
winter colour, 11, 15, 48, 156
wisteria, **82**, 147, 194
witch hazel, **51**
withering of foliage, 11
woodrush, giant, 172

Xanthoceras, 163, **165**

yew, common, 188
　creeping, 95
　golden, 189
　golden Irish, 69, 71, **72**, 189
　Irish, 53, **56**, 57, 189
yulan, 171

zinnia, 69